SCOTTISH ARMS
AND
ARMOUR

SHIRE PUBLICATIONS

SCOTTISH ARMS AND ARMOUR

FERGUS CANNAN

SHIRE PUBLICATIONS

Published in Great Britain in 2009 by Shire Publications Ltd, Midland House, West Way, Botley, Oxford OX2 0PH, United Kingdom.

443 Park Avenue South, New York, NY 10016, USA.

E-mail: shire@shirebooks.co.uk   ·   www.shirebooks.co.uk

A CIP catalgoue record for this book is available from the Bristish Library.

Shire Collections no. 1   .   ISBN-978 0 74780 698 1

Fergus Cannan has asserted his right under the copyright, Designs and Patents Act, 1998, to be identified as the author of this book.

Designed by Ken Vail Graphic Design, Cambridge, UK and Typset in Bembo.

Printed in Malta by Gutenberg Press Ltd.

09 10 11 12 13   10 9 8 7 6 5 4 3 2 1

COVER IMAGE
Hilt of a Highland two-handed sword of the early sixteenth century (British Museum)

PAGE 2 IMAGE
Hilt of a Lowland two-handed sword, mid sixteenth century (Peter Finer Antique Arms and Armour).

DEDICATION
I dedicate this book to my wife Heather, love of my life.

ACKNOWLEDGEMENTS
First, I must record my heartfelt thanks to the assessors of the Authors' Foundation, who awarded me a generous grant while I wrote this book. I owe a real debt to Michael German and Dominic Strickland, Michael German Antiques; Linda Fairlie and Gillian Simison, East Ayrshire Arts and Museums; James Charles Macnab of Macnab; Mairi Mooney and Fiona Mawick, West Highland Museum; Angus Patterson, Victoria and Albert Museum; John and Philip Spooner, West Street Antiques; and to Nick Wright at Shire for being such a professional and friendly commissioning editor. My thanks also to Cormac Bourke, Ulster Museum; David Caldwell, National Museums of Scotland; Thomas Del Mar; the staff of Dumfries Museum; Peter and Redmond Finer; Liam Fitchett, LM RFC; Rachel Hunt, Cothele; Roy King, Sussex Farm Museum; Linda Montgomery, Trinity College Dublin; M. Mooney and J. M. Egan, Carlisle City Council; Tim Newark, *Military Illustrated*; Fergus Tickell, Northern Energy Developments; Morag Traynor, City Lit; Commodore Christopher Waite and Terry Stefaniw, Worshipful Company of Armourers and Brasiers; Clem Webb, Museum of the London Scottish Regiment; Lesley Whitelaw, Honourable Society of the Middle Temple. Special mention has to be made of my mother Crescy and my friend Ethan Hayes Kalemjian, with whom I have had many discussions about Scottish history. Both have proofread parts of the book, as did my wife – thank you to you all.

CONTENTS

FOREWORD

WITH its violent and war-torn history, the impact of arms and armour and their production in both the Highlands and Lowlands of Scotland cannot be exaggerated. It is therefore surprising that so few scholars of Scottish history have paid anything but passing attention to the subject; all the more so when we know that, at least in the Highlands, the ancient armourers and smiths were highly regarded men of some status in their communities. For those of us interested in Scottish history, this book fills a gap and provides us with a deeper understanding.

In Chapter 3 there is a mention among others of the Macnabs of Barachastlain. I have fond memories of Iain Macnab, who in 1958 was recognised by the Lord Lyon King of Arms as 'Representer of Barachastlain, the ancient Armourers and Standard-bearers of the Chief.' Iain was an artist and engraver, who would have liked to have been a sculptor, but wounds suffered in the First World War precluded this. He always maintained that his skill as an engraver was inherited from his Highland ancestors. Some fifty years ago he painted a picture of the Macnab burial ground on the island of Innis Bhuidhe in the Falls of Dochart at Killin, which he gave me as a wedding present. It occupies a prominent place in our house. Iain, as were his ancestors, was a 'man of art.'

Fergus Cannan's interest in his own family history led to a study of Scottish history and arms and armour. He was born in London in 1978. His ancestors were lairds in Glenkens. They were both Covenanters and Jacobites. One ancestor was Sir John Wedderburn, last Baronet of Blackness, who for his part in the 'Forty-Five was executed in 1746 on Kennington Common. Another ancestor was Princess Mary, daughter of King James II of Scotland; thus he can claim descent from the Bruce. He is also descended on one side of his family from the branch of MacGregors that comes off the Chiefly line with Gregor the Handsome (d. 1415). As a scholar, he became tired of hearing nonsense about Scottish history, and also of Scottish arms and armour being ignored by historians, who usually claim that there is nothing to study. His myth-busting approach to history, particularly Scottish, is to be welcomed!

In this book, Fergus Cannan has provided us with a considered, critical study of the physical military heritage of both Highland and Lowland Scots, who as soldiers have had an impact in wars across the globe out of all proportion to the small size of their country. To all those with an interest in Scottish history I commend this book.

James Charles Macnab of Macnab
The Macnab
23rd Chief of Clan Macnab

Chapter One

THE BEGINNINGS OF SCOTTISH ARMS AND ARMOUR

LANDSCAPE and climate are important forces to consider as we open the door on this monumental topic, for if ever a people has been shaped by its geography, it is the Scots. Nearly three-quarters of their country is mountain or high hill, and all year round the weather is harsh and temperamental. Much of the landscape is too rugged to sustain anything more than the most frugal ways of life; only something like 8 per cent of the country makes for good pasturing. The earliest evidence for settlement in Scotland dates from about 8,500 BC. These first settlers were hunter-gatherers who probably migrated from continental Europe, perhaps while Britain was still joined with the European mainland. They led a nomadic life, trapping and hunting, moving along the lochs and rivers in canoes. Their only weapons were made from stone, horn, bone or wood. Some five thousand years later, a few settled communities based on subsistence crop farming emerged in Scotland, but most of the people remained hunters, fishermen and herders.

Scottish axe-heads of stone, dating between 2200 and 1500 BC. The example on the left is of greenstone and was found at Longniddry, East Lothian; the axe-head in the centre is serpentine, and was found at Portpatrick, Wigtownshire; on the right, a perforated granite axe-head, found at Chapelton, Ayrshire. (The Trustees of the National Museums of Scotland)

CELTIC SCOTLAND

With the passing of another three and a half millennia, we learn of the 'Caledonians'. They were a confederation of Celts rather than a single tribe, whose homelands stretched across the Highlands. Cassius Dio (*c.* AD 150–235) describes the *Caledonii* (a Latin rather than native term) as living simply on flocks, game and fruit. Dio praises their ability to endure cold, hunger and hardship. Cornelius Tacitus (born *c.* AD 55) grants us a precious glimpse of vanished lives by telling us what the Caledonians looked like – 'reddish hair and large limbs'. From Roman sources – the Celts of Scotland themselves kept no written records – a picture emerges of a hardy and indomitable, if impulsive and wild people. They were clearly remarkable fighters, and it speaks volumes that the Caledonians, located on the very edge of the known world with few resources and little foreign trade, should be included in the Verona List of AD 312–14 as one of the Empire's most stubborn enemies.

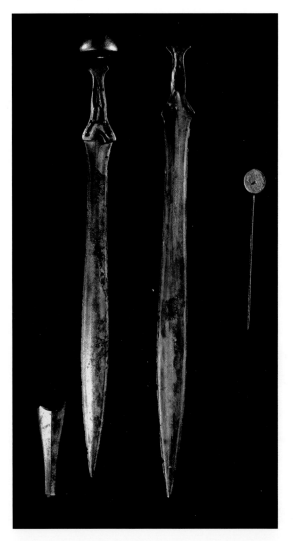

An arms horde of the late Bronze Age found at Tarves, Grampian, and consisting of two swords, a pommel, scabbard chape and clothes pin; c. 1000–850 BC (The Trustees of the British Museum).

At the close of Scottish prehistory, small-scale wars raged across the countryside as Celtic tribes feuded and vied for regional power. Their wars were not fought by professional soldiers but rather on the basis that every male was a fighter, and by and large he was. Sometimes the women were too. The weapons and armour used by these proto-Scotsmen reflected the age-old Celtic belief that war was a sacred contest of wills, pitting man against man, honour against honour. Single combat was the Celt's forte, though he was also skilled at tracking and laying ambushes. Archaeology suggests that ownership of weapons was widespread. While the bearing of arms was clearly an important mark of free manhood, the basic armament of the ordinary warrior – the spear and shield – was also used for hunting, and his knife was likewise not only a weapon but an everyday essential.

Archaeology also shows that the Celts of Scotland were extraordinarily accomplished smiths. The Bronze Age had reached Scotland around 2000 BC, enabling smiths to make heavy swords for slashing with elegant teardrop-shaped blades. They also made helmets from bronze, and broad spearheads, magnificent torcs, massive bracelets, armlets and brooches, as well as shields of wood, covered (almost certainly) in leather. Missile fire on the battlefield was provided by slings, short-bows, throwing axes and javelins. Decorative weapons and exquisite shields of sheet bronze were also made, and cast into rivers and lakes as offerings to the gods.

WARRIORS OF IRON

In about 800–700 BC the Iron Age began in Scotland. Iron is harder and more resilient than bronze and so better for making weapons and armour. Until about the third century BC, iron swords were short and stubby, but improvements in metalworking gave rise to very long swords in the second and first centuries. Swords were carried in metal scabbards handsomely ornamented with enamel-work, and slung from belts or chains down the right (as opposed to left) leg. Tacitus says that swords in Scotland had blunt tips, and archaeology confirms that they remained throughout the Iron Age weapons for cutting, not thrusting. The coming of iron also meant the appearance of the two-handed axe in Scotland – a far more fearsome weapon than the earlier bronze pole-axe – together with giant broadleaf spearheads of iron, and, for the noblemen of the tribe, iron helmets (although bronze helmets were still made). Helmets commonly had animal crests (the boar was especially revered by Celts for its great strength), often with hinged cheek-pieces similar to those used by the Romans. Together with their armour, they wore woollen tunics or vests with trousers (but not yet the kilt), woven in variegated tartan or tweed-like checks.

An axe-wielding man, from a Pictish carving at Barflat.

Conjectural map of territories of the Scottish tribes, c. AD 100–200, according to the names given them by Classical writers.

Section of replica mail showing how each link is riveted.

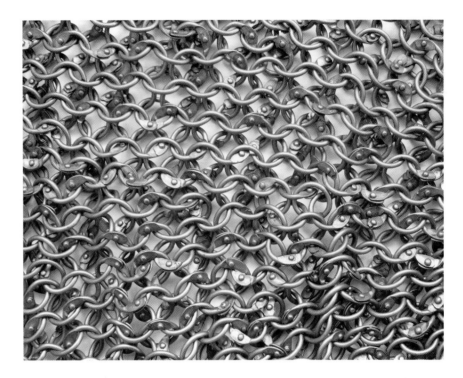

THE TOOLS OF DEFENCE AND ATTACK

As iron-working began in Scotland, hill-forts sprang up across the landscape. These were smaller than the massive feats of earthwork in southern England, but the basic idea was the same: a timber stockade, with deep excavated ditches and steep banks of compacted soil constructed on top of a well-chosen hill. Around 300 BC stone forts – *dun* in Gaelic (hence Dunbar, Dunvegan, etc.) – began to be built, followed some two hundred years later by the ingenious *broch* or dry-stone tower, and *crannog* island fort. With the advent of forts, the sling came into its own as a weapon. These simple weapons, made only from a thong of leather, should not be underestimated. Their stones (about 3 cm across) could wound or kill at 60 metres, and a group of men armed with them could easily lay down a deadly barrage from the ramparts of a hill-fort.

Most warriors fought on foot, but some rode into battle in war chariots. The chariot had been given up by continental European armies by the middle of the third century BC, but in Britain and Ireland they continued to be used for hundreds of years. There was sense in the retention of this old, versatile weapon, which could be used for hit-and-run attacks, for reconnaissance and for harrying lines of enemy infantry. Tacitus says the Caledonian chariots were 'terrifying' at Mons Graupius in AD 83/4 – even when rough ground and dense ranks of men brought the chariots to a halt, the Romans found 'runaway chariots and riderless horses came plunging into their ranks from all sides.'

Around the same time that chariots vanished from continental European warfare, mail armour appeared. Often called 'chain mail', it consists of small metal rings linked together to make a woven mesh almost as flexible as cloth. No tools survive from the period, but it is likely that mail was made by drawing soft iron wire around a cylindrical metal rod, and then cut into separate rings. The ends of each ring were flattened and pierced to allow a wedge-shaped rivet to fasten the ring shut, and the garment was slowly built up, with four rings linked through each one. Case-hardening (surface toughening of metal by heating it for hours while packed in charcoal or other organic material) or quench-hardening (heating and rapid cooling in water) was required to give the mail enough strength to fend off blows from weapons. As long as the rings are riveted, the degree of protection mail offers is high, though it can be punctured by arrows or by a concerted thrust from a spear.

Given that the earliest known mail comes from continental Celtic graves of the third century BC, it is fairly likely to have been a Celtic innovation. It is surely significant that in Gaelic the word for a mail shirt is *luireach*, while the same garment in Latin is *lorica*. The latter language probably provides the origin of the term (unless they are both derived from a now lost Indo-European root), but the Romans are said to have copied the mail armour they saw on the noblemen of Gaul – another Celtic people – right down to the distinctive cape-like defence for the shoulders. It is reasonable to suppose that mail was used in Scotland, since other surviving metalwork from Scotland shows native smiths had the necessary high level of skill. If so, a shirt of mail would have been, as in Gaul, the preserve of the nobility since it requires many hours of work, and was an expensive item. As for the rank and file, the evidence from later Pictish stone carvings is that tunics of stiffened or padded leather were used, and it is hard to believe these were not used by their forebears.

Nearly every man carried a shield. After protecting the warrior during the charge, the shield took on an offensive dimension, as the Celt used it to sweep at his opponent, shoving him backwards, fighting in a berserk two-handed action. The shields of the continental Celts were often man-sized, but in Scotland they were, if sculptural depictions are anything to go by, almost buckler-like and occasionally analogous to the later 'targe'. Tacitus describes the shields used by the Caledonians and their allies at Mons Graupius as 'small', contrasting them to the large defensive type used by the Romans. Sculpture generally represents the shields of the Celts in Scotland as square, round or oblong. Archaeology suggests they were made from planks of chamfered wood, centred on an iron (or occasionally wooden) boss, and bands, again of iron, reinforced the edges. The exterior of the shield was probably covered in leather and painted or tooled with stylised geometric and symbolic emblems. Behind the boss on the back of the shield was an oval or round cavity for the hand, which would grip a single horizontal handle made of wood, probably reinforced with iron bracing.

Celtic helmet, c. AD 50–150, said to have been found in northern Britain. Made from copper alloy with repoussé ornament on the neck; the cross-hatched domes were originally covered with opaque red glass. (The Trustees of the British Museum)

Warrior, possibly a chieftain, on a Pictish slab from the Brough of Biscay.

THE TUMULT OF WAR

Without question, aggressiveness and intimidation were the main armour of the early Scottish warrior: attack was his defence. A key implement for the inducement of terror in enemies was the 'carnyx', a trumpet-like instrument held vertically when played. Diodorus Siculus notes, in the first century BC, the use of this 'peculiar barbarian' instrument by the Gauls, who 'blow into them and produce a harsh sound which suits the tumult of war.' One of the best surviving examples was found in a peat bog with other offerings in Deskford, near Leitchiston in Banffshire, in around 1816. This haunting object is the head or 'bell' of a carnyx and takes the form of a boar, already noted as a symbol of physical power for the Celts. Like the war-pipes of a later age, the carnyx was designed both to unnerve the enemy, and to fire up the men whose harsh bray it rallied. Polybius writes vividly of the 'dreadful din' of the advancing Cisalpine Gauls at Telamon, Italy, in 225 BC, for they had 'innumerable trumpeters and horn-blowers', added to which the 'whole army were shouting their war-cries', creating such 'a tumult of sound that it seemed that not only the trumpeters and the soldiers but all the country round had got a voice and caught up the cry.'

Just as terrifying, Polybius continues, were the 'appearance and the gestures of the naked warriors' in the Celtic front ranks at Telamon. All were 'in the prime of life, and finely built men, and all in the leading companies richly adorned with gold torcs and armlets.' This could easily be a description of the Celts of Scotland, who would often strip to the waist to fight, wearing only baggy checked trews; others would forgo clothes altogether, covering their skin in blue patterns of woad. There was an element of practical sense to this heroic nudity, in that wounds were less likely to become infected than those inflicted on a man wearing dirty, germ-ridden clothes. But this benefit was largely incidental to the purpose of nakedness, which was to show that a warrior was protected by divine forces and that he was devoid of fear in the face of death.

THE COMING OF ROME

The shock charge was the only battlefield tactic the Celts really cared for. In the moments before the charge, blood lust inflamed the throngs of fighters. The strange call of the carnyx would signal the charge and a mass of infantry and chariots would rush headlong at the enemy and attempt to crash through and break up his battle-lines. Thereafter, the chiefs and their men could do little more than put their faith in the gods and hope for the best. Against ill-trained or ill-disciplined troops, the Celtic charge was unstoppable. The Romans were a different matter.

Military operations against Britannia (its inhabitants are more likely to have called it Albion) began in the late summer of 55 BC when Julius Caesar led two legions across the Channel in revenge for British support for the Gauls. The following year Caesar returned with a larger force. Venturing into the interior of southern England, he met stiff resistance. Autumn approached and the legionaries were evacuated homewards. Then, in AD 43, the Emperor Claudius dispatched a massive Roman army to Britain. Years of bitter campaigning followed in England and Wales before Gnaeus Julius Agricola, governor of Britain, attempted an invasion of Scotland in about AD 80.

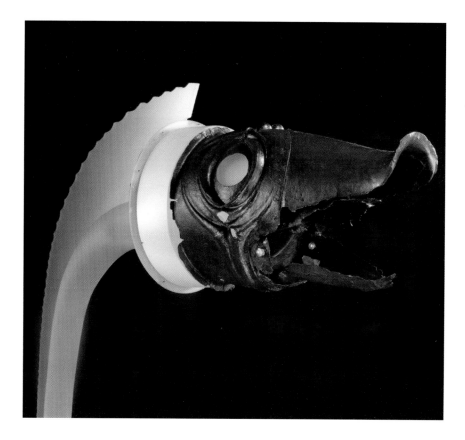

Head of a 'carnyx' or battle trumpet in the form of a boar, found at Deskford in Banffshire. Beaten bronze with brass fittings, c. AD 100–300. (The Trustees of the National Museums of Scotland)

Three or four years later at Mons Graupius in the north of Scotland (possibly just outside Perth) a reported 30,000 Caledonians and north Britons clashed with 20,000 Romans. Tacitus, Agricola's son-in-law, describes the encounter as beginning with an exchange of missiles, after which Roman auxiliaries (themselves often 'barbarians') attacked the British forces. In the tight press of bodies, there was not enough space for the Britons to make proper use of what Tacitus calls their 'unwieldy', 'huge' swords. The Romans were armed with the neat *gladius*, and to make matters worse the Romans' shields were, conversely, much larger than the small British shields. After 'raining blow after blow', the auxiliaries got the better of the Britons. The British chariots, meanwhile, were routed, and warriors stationed on a hillside coming to the aid of their comrades were 'turned back in disorder.' Tacitus remarks sternly: 'The tactics of the Britons now turned against them,' and claims that 10,000 perished in exchange for 360 Roman lives. This was obviously a catastrophic defeat.

However, the Caledonians had the upper hand when it came to guerrilla war, and the Highlands, as always, remained impossible to subdue. Only a few years after Mons Graupius, a new legionary base at Inchtuthil by Perth had to be abandoned while still under construction, and all the territory beyond the Forth was given up. Hadrian's Wall, built after Emperor Hadrian's visit to Britain in AD 122, though an impressive visual statement of power, is an admission of this failure. The Wall was no more than a defensive marker to a frightening hinterland; at any rate, the Caledonians stormed

Carnyx-men as depicted on the Gunderstrup cauldron, first or second century BC.

RIGHT
A Pictish warrior depicted by a Pictish sculptor. From the Collesie stone.

FAR RIGHT
Clear evidence for the use of the crossbow by the Picts, here employed by a huntsman. From a cross-slab at St Vigean's Museum, Angus.

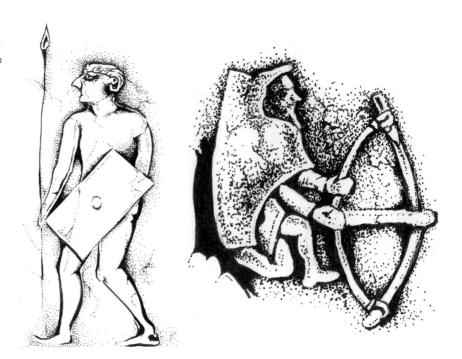

it a number of times. The hasty retreat of Roman rule preserved Scotland as a fastness for old Celtic military traditions – a point of incalculable significance for the development of Scottish arms and armour.

LAND OF THE PAINTED ONES

First mentioned by Eumenius in AD 297, the Picts were a loose grouping of northern tribes made up of the earlier Caledonians and others. Their name would seem to mean 'the painted ones' and is possibly their own nickname for themselves, presumably an allusion to their taste for body-painting. Gildas (fl. *c.* 475–*c.* 550), himself a Briton, claims 'marauding Picts' had more hair on their faces than clothes on their bodies. Even so, we can see from their sculpture that the Picts used the crossbow, as well as cavalry armed with lances, and that they sometimes wore long tunics, perhaps incorporating some form of padding. While nakedness and war paint survived, there comes a point in Pictish sculpture when we can suddenly see what look like 'medieval' Scottish warriors. Christianity had now also arrived, traditionally in the form of St Ninian (*c.* AD 360–432) and St Columba (AD 521–97), though St Patrick (*c.* 389–*c.* 461) found at least some of the Picts 'shameful, wicked and apostate.'

Unfortunately for the Picts, they came under severe pressure from a Gaelic-speaking Celtic people from Antrim in Ireland whom the Classical writers call *Scotti*. Around AD 500, Fergus the Great established the 'Scottish' kingdom of Dál Riata, in present day Argyll. This heady age of transition was compounded by fighting between the regional kings of southern Scotland and northern England, and from *c.* AD 780 the Vikings became a menace. Most dramatic of all these events occurred in AD 842/3 when Fergus's descendant, Kenneth MacAlpin, seized the Pictish throne, uniting the Picts and the Scots, paving the way for 'Alba', or in English, 'Scotland.'

OPPOSITE
A Scottish warrior from the Book of Kells, *probably made in the late eighth century AD on Iona. (The Board of Trinity College Dublin)*

filiatt est tu es filius meus dilectus in te·
bene· complacuit mihi·

Ipse ihserat incipiens quasi an
norum triginta· ut putabatur filius

ioseph

VI	fuit	heli
VI	fuit	matha
VI	fuit	leui
VI	fuit	melchi
VI	fuit	iannne
VI	fuit	ioseph
VI	fuit	mathat hie
VI	fuit	amos
VI	fuit	nauum
VI	fuit	esli
VI	fuit	nagge
VI	fuit	enaath

Chapter Two

THE MIDDLE AGES

MEDIEVAL SCOTLAND was a predominantly Celtic land. The north and west, from Galloway in the south to the Orkneys in the north, to Perth in the east, were heavily Celtic and Norse – this was Scotland's *Gàidhealtachd*. Lothian in the south-east came under the influence of Saxon and Norman settlers, but rather than bringing radically new ideas about warfare these newcomers settled into existing Scottish military traditions, even if they usually stopped short of adopting the Gaelic language. Among the Gaelic Scots, a strong cultural solidarity existed with their fellow Gaels – the Irish and Manx – making for a fluid exchange of military technologies, and also soldiers. All Scots had weapons in their homes, and every male was supposed to attend regular *wappinschaws* – 'weapon-shows' or parades of arms. Few did, but when the call to arms went out, Scotland was routinely able to field large armies of hardened and self-reliant, though often raw and unpolished, fighting men. In his *Historie and Cronicles of Scotland*, Robert Lindsay of Pitscottie (*c.* 1532–80) records the drama of the marshalling of men and equipment in 1547 as a proclamation was made, ordering:

> … all maner of man betuix sextie and sextene baitht sprituall and temporall, the father allis weill as the sone, gif he war abill, to compeir at Edinburgh in thair best airmour and array witht xxx dayis wictuall to pase with governour and to defend the realme fre the Inglischmen.

SIDES OF IRON

It was this kind of 'civilian' army that David I raised for his invasion of England in the twelfth century. The *Gesta Stephani*, written by an English contemporary, says King David 'published an edict' and amassed an enormous army of 'barbarous and unclean' men, who were 'neither subdued by bitter cold nor stunted by severe hunger'. The men of Galloway are alleged to have been particularly wild. They formed a substantial section of King David's army at Northallerton in 1138, the famous 'Battle of the Standard.' Like most of David's men, the Gallovidians were scantily dressed and nearly all infantry. The *Gesta Stephani* notes the Scots in general 'rely on swift feet and light armour'. They were also trouserless. A few wore hose (*osain* in Gaelic) in diced checks or mottled tartans, but the nickname of 'redshank' would stick for a reason.

King David had some knights in heavy armour at Northallerton, but the Galloway contingent took offence at the suggestion that the honour of being first into battle should fall to another. St Ailred (1109–67), an adviser to David, says the Gallovidians insisted they did not need armour as they had 'iron sides, a breast of bronze' and 'a mind void of fear'. David yielded to the Galloway men, who 'gave vent thrice to a yell of horrible sound' and took off across the field in a classic display of Scottish gusto.

OPPOSITE
An imagined view of the Earl of Montrose (centre) at Flodden in 1513, clad in German armour. On the left is one of a group of men-at-arms sent by the King of France. On the right is a Scottish gentleman in half-armour with a 'pavise' shield. In the background is a Border 'reiver' in a jack. (Painting by Graham Turner)

The rest of the Scottish army charged, but the English lines held. After a time, the English 'shower of arrows' and the 'swords of the knights', tells Ailred, became too much, and rallying his men to his standard, David conducted a fighting retreat.

GALLÓGLAIGH

The Scots' use of light armour was to some extent vindicated by victory over the English in 1141, after which Northumbria was ruled by Scotland for sixteen years. Even so, the experience of fighting heavily armoured English knights and being fired on by massed archers must have been harrowing. One solution lay in the legacy of the Norsemen, a people with a stunning record for the making of high-quality axes, swords, helmets and mail shirts. Their most explicit heirs – both militarily and genetically – were the *gallóglaigh*.

First mentioned by the Irish annalists in the mid-thirteenth century, 'galloglass' ('foreign warriors' in Gaelic) were Hebridean mercenaries armed with two-handed axes who served in the retinues of Irish warlords. Once in Ireland, they established mighty warrior kindreds of MacCabes, MacDonnells, MacDowells, MacRorys, MacSheehys and MacSweeneys. The heroic size of their axes can be seen in John Derricke's *Image of Irelande* (published in 1581), where galloglass in mail shirts and corrugated helmets are shown hotly engaged with English halberdiers. Sir Anthony St Leger (*c.* 1496–1559), Lord Deputy of Ireland, recalls galloglass were typically 'harnessed in mayle and bassenettes', adding that 'these sorte of men be those that doo not lightly abandon the fielde, but byde the brunte to the deathe.'

LUIREACH AGUS CLOGAD

In Ireland the galloglass's equipment – summarised neatly in 1428 in the register of John Swayne, Primate of Ireland, as 'owry [every] man acton habirchon pischane basnete', and as late as 1610 by the old campaigner Barnaby Rich as 'a Scull, a shirt of mail and a Galloglass Axe' – made them a novelty. In western Scotland this combination of mail armour, open-faced helmet and large weapon was conventional attire for the Gaelic gentleman or *duine-uasal*. The same equipment is given human personality in a song composed by the warrior-bard Do'ull MacIain 'ic Sheumais (d. 1650), who speaks of 'the three heroes [*tri seòid*]' of 'mail shirt, and helmet, and sword [*luireach, is clogad, is claidheamh*]' that he has passed to his son-in-law. The Gaelic panoply of arms is as memorably evident in the *Book of Clanranald*, a collection of stories assembled by bards of that clan, in which we read of a warrior donning the 'armour of conflict and strife', the principal item being a 'beautifully wrought' mail shirt, ornamented with gold and 'brilliant Danish gems'.

The mail shirt (in Gaelic *luireach*) takes centre stage in the Highland arsenal from the time of the Vikings until the seventeenth century. John Mair or Major (*c.* 1467–1550) in his *History of Greater Britain* says that in 'time of war' Highlanders 'cover the

Seal of King David I of Scotland (reigned 1124–53). The son of Malcolm III and St Margaret, it is not by chance that David is portrayed as a Norman knight. His wife was the great-niece of William the Conqueror, and he encouraged Norman nobles to settle in Scotland. David's achievement was maintaining peaceful coexistence between the newcomers and traditional Celtic elites. (John Wesley's House and the Museum of Methodism)

Single-handed Highland sword of the fifteenth century, found at Glenshee, Perthshire. (The Trustees of the National Museums of Scotland)

An illustration from John Derricke's Image of Irelande *(1581) showing galloglass pushed back by English halberdiers and hand-gunners. Their piper ('Pyper') is among the dead.(University of Edinburgh)*

whole body with a coat of mail, made of iron rings [*loricam ex ferris*], and in it they fight.' Robert Lindsay of Pitscottie uses the Old French *haubergeon* for mail shirt when he writes that Highlanders mustering in 1542 all appeared with 'haberjouns and twa handit swordis, quhilk [which] was the airmor of the hielandis men'. John Lesley (1527–96), Bishop of Ross, says exactly the same in his *Historie of Scotland*: 'For defence', Highlanders 'used a coat of mail woven in iron rings'. George Buchannan (1506–82), James VI's tutor, confirms this impression still further in his own history of Scotland, remarking on the great length of the Highland *luireach*: 'Their armour wherewith they cover their bodies in time of warre, is an iron bonnet and an habbergion side almost even to their heels.'

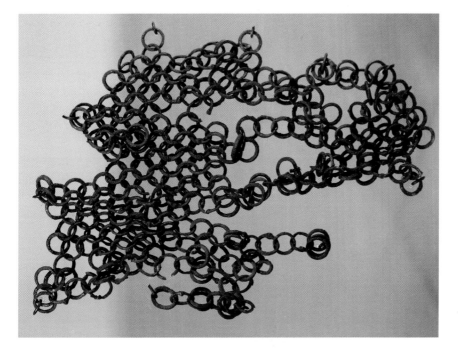

Portion of iron mail armour, recorded in 1866 as found in peat or clay near Moffat; later recorded as found near Loch Carlingwark. Threave Castle is close to Loch Carlingwark and belonged to the powerful Douglas family.
(Dumfries Museum, www.futuremuseum.co.uk)

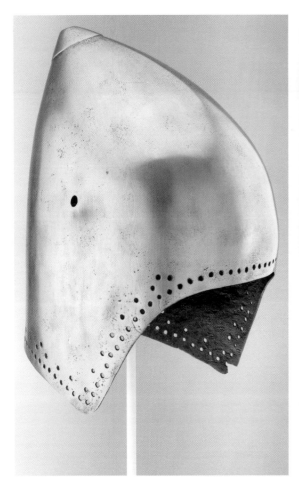

In Scotland's Celtic west, many warriors wore mantles of mail (a *pisane* to the Englishman John Swayne), often with tall, pointed helmets of the sort generally identified in English as a 'basinet', or alternatively a simple conical 'spanglehelm', with or without a nose guard. In Gaelic these are both a *clogad*. Helmets across Scotland were much the same: in 1318 Robert the Bruce (reigned 1306–29) ordered every man worth £10 in goods to have, among other equipment, a 'basnet', while in the margins of the Carlisle Charter of 1316 – granted in recognition of the citizens' determined defence against a siege by the Scots the year before – one Scot wears what may be interpreted as a kettle-hat (or bonnet), another possibly a rudimentary pot-helmet; others appear to have only hoods and capes. In the sixteenth century, Borderers, Lowlanders and galloglass made use of Italian 'morions', 'cabassets' and 'burgonets'. Highlanders also often wore imported helmets; helmets were apparently made in Scotland but no obviously Scottish-made examples survive. Nonetheless, the evidence from tomb figures and other graphic and written sources is consistent and clear that most Scots preferred open-faced helmets, whether domed or cone-shaped, of the sort encapsulated by Rich as a 'Skull'.

ACTOUNS

Mail armour was useless without some kind of padding to dampen the shock of blows to the body. We therefore find the warrior in the *Book of Clanranald* wears beneath his *luireach* a 'handsome, well-fitting, rich, highly-embroidered, beautiful, many coloured, artfully done, gusseted, corded' jerkin, to 'guard him against dangers.' Lesley notes Highlanders wore mail 'over a leather jerkin, stout and of handsome appearance, which we call an acton', just as Hector Boece (*c.* 1465–1536) speaks of (supposedly ancient) Scots in his *History of Scotland* as dressed in 'habergeons, sum of irne, sum of leddir, commonly callit nactouns.' The 'actoun', as it was known in Scots English (Irish *cotún*, English *aketon*, from Arabic *al-qutn*, 'cotton'), was typically a long leather or linen coat with vertically stitched quilting stuffed with wool. In his vignette of Highland military apparel, Major reveals to us its layered construction: 'The common folk among the wild Scots [*vulgus sylvestrium*] rush into battle having their whole body clad in a linen garment manifoldly sewed and painted or daubed with pitch, and with a covering of deerskin.'

This made for a very thick, multi-layered coat that was warm and water-resistant from waxing and pitching, as well as highly protective – it had to be, since it was often the only armour the Scottish soldier had. Bruce's ruling of 1318 in fact stipulates that men worth £10 are to have an actoun or mail coat, not necessarily both. They are also to have a sword, spear, basinet and 'gluffis of playt'; those owning chattels to the value of a cow are asked only to have 'a gud sper or a gud bow with a schaff of arowys'. A parliamentary act of 1429–30 includes 'doublets of fence' as required equipment for

OPPOSITE RIGHT
Helmet in Dean Castle, Kilmarnock, bearing a Milanese armourer's mark, with mail neck guard lined with leather; fifteenth century. This is exactly the kind of simple but practical helmet used by medieval Scots. (East Ayrshire Arts and Museums, www.futuremuseum.co.uk)

The Carlisle Charter of 1316. The embellishment of the letter 'E' was the work of a local scribe and shows Scottish soldiers laying siege to the city. The English knight wearing the crested great helm can be identified by his shield as Sir Andrew Harclay (d. 1323). Harclay clearly learnt from the Scots, for in 1322 he led infantry, says Lanercost, arrayed 'in the Scottish fashion' against the earls of Hereford and Lancaster at Boroughbridge. (By kind permission of Carlisle City Council and Cumbria County Record Office)

Bannockburn, 1314. Bannockburn was the turning point in Scotland's war for freedom from English domination, and demonstrated the resilience, discipline and killing-power of Scottish infantry when led by a commander of the calibre of Robert the Bruce and his three legendary lieutenants James Douglas, Thomas Randolph and younger brother Edward Bruce. (Painting by Graham Turner)

'zemen' (yeomen), and for much of the Middle Ages the actoun was extensively used throughout Scotland. By the end of the fifteenth century most Lowlanders had given up wearing actouns, but they remained much used by warriors in the Gaelic west – Highlanders, Islanders and galloglass – for another hundred years.

COATS OF PLATE

It was the 'coat of plates' or 'jack', another cheap, flexible and efficient form of armour, which became the mark of the Lowlander and Borderer in the late Middle Ages. First mentioned in the late fourteenth century, the jack consisted of two or three layers of quilted twill, canvas or linen, between which square metal plates were riveted or threaded into place. Most were waist-length and sleeveless, though longer varieties are noted in an act of 1481, which requires jacks to reach the knee if worn without leg armour. Some were worn with mail sleeves, others with plate 'splints'. The Englishman William Patten (d. 1580) spotted Scots at the battle of Pinkie in 1547 with 'chains of latten drawn four or five times along the thighs of their hosen, and doublet sleeves' to protect against cuts – 'of that I saw many.'

Lowland and Border lairds wore jacks as much as the common man. Patten remembers the Scots at Pinkie as being 'all clad a lyke in Jackes covered in whyte leather, with doublets of the same or of fustian'. Even the Earl of Arran, co-commander of the Scots army, was wearing one, albeit with a purple velvet cover. Patten blames the rather meagre appearance of the Scots nobles, their 'lack of brooch, ring, or garment of silk' and general 'vileness of port', for their high death rate at Pinkie, since the English could not identify those worth capturing and ransoming.

THE IMPORTANCE OF ATTACK

Though quick and unencumbered, the Scots were terribly vulnerable to attack from arrows or firearms. Stationary blocks of Scots spearmen were destroyed in a storm of arrows at Falkirk (1298) and Homildon Hill (1402). Abbot Walter Bower (1385–1449) speaks of the Scots at Homildon as 'smothered with arrows', their hands nailed to their spears. Thousands died as pointlessly at Dupplin Moor (1332) and Neville's Cross (1346). It was the English and Welsh longbow that was most feared, and it is understandable that Scotsmen – from above and below the Highland Line – would almost always attempt to close with the enemy as quickly as possible.

It was in a fast, furious clash that the Scots fared best, though the results of this daring, volatile tactic were mixed. At Faughart (1318) Edward Bruce, in an action that cost him his life, attacked before his army was formed up, allowing the English to defeat the Scots and their Irish allies piecemeal. At Halidon Hill (1333), too, the Scots showed zest if not foresight when they attempted to attack English archers up hill and across a marsh, leading to appalling slaughter and more than half their cavalry being killed or wounded.

However, when James IV was killed fighting in the front row of pikemen at Flodden (1513), a pike in his hands like any other soldier, he was only doing what was expected of any Scottish commander. The tactic of getting to hand-blows as soon as the opportunity arose could work fantastically, as at the River Sark (1448), when a Lowland-Borders army 'wes sa inrageit' (says Pitscottie) that it rushed 'furieouslie' upon the 'Inglisch wangaird' before the English could get into position. It was the initial impact of the charge that did most damage, Pitscottie writing that at Sark 'great slaughter' was made at the 'first tocoming' – so much so that the English were pushed 'cleane abak fre their standart', before breaking and fleeing.

It is well to remember that the Highlands, Lowlands and Borders alike were hard and unruly places governed by violent clans. All three regions were inhabited by gritty men who had often seen much blood spilt before they stepped on to the battlefield. The men themselves were frightening enough – Thomas Ruthal, Bishop of Durham, wrote in late 1513 that the Scots at Flodden had been 'such large and strong men, they would not fall when four or five bills struck one of them'. John Dymmok, an Elizabethan who served in Ireland, trembles as he thinks of galloglass, 'men of great and mighty bodies, cruel without compassion.' Just as awe-struck was Don Pedro de Ayala, Spanish ambassador to the Scottish court in 1498, who saw the Western Islesmen in action and could only say: 'They do not know what danger is.'

Psychology played a large part in the Scottish art of war. Jean Froissart (*c.* 1337– *c.* 1410) says the Scottish infantry carried 'horns slung from their neck' and 'big

Recreated English longbowmen of the fifteenth century. (The Erpyngham Retinue photographed by Adam Monaghan)

drums' at Otterburn (1388), which their commanders ordered them to play because the noise 'gives them a tremendous thrill and strikes terror into their enemies' – and the Scots did indeed prevail that day. At Myton (1319) the Scots used smoke to cloak their movements, a tactic repeated, though without success, at Flodden. At Pinkie the Scots attempted to scare the horses of the English with rattles, a device Patten calls 'witless' and unable to 'duddle' the English or their horses. Nonetheless, the Scots were always ready to experiment, and after firearms made the battleground a noisier place in the sixteenth century, war-pipes became a leading weapon in the war of nerves. So too was the human voice. In 1327 Sir James Douglas (d. 1330) raided northern England, and Froissart relates that at night Douglas's men 'always lit great fires and raised such a din by blowing on their horns and whooping in chorus that it sounded to the English as though all the devils in hell had been let loose.'

YELLOW WAR-COATS

The giant saffron-coloured 'war-coat', at once a tunic and belted-plaid, was, meanwhile, something only found in the Highlands and Islands. Major mentions this peculiar garment, saying that Highlanders in his day were naked 'the mid leg to the foot' and that 'their dress, is for an overgarment, a loose plaid and a shirt dyed with saffron [*camisia croco tincta*]'. In Gaelic it was called the *lèine croich* ('saffron shirt') in respect of its rich golden hue, a colour still used for the kilts of some Irish regiments today. The common clansman probably obtained this colour from crushed bark, leaves, salt and urine, but Lesley claims real saffron – an expensive and exotic spice derived from the saffron crocus, which only grows in hot climes – was indeed used by 'the rich'. Martin Martin, a native of Skye writing around 1695, agrees that 'Persons of Distinction' wore shirts 'dyed with that Herb'. Clearly, it was the use of saffron, together with the amount of cloth used, which marked the shirts of commoners from that of the nobility, a divide perhaps implicit in a description of Angus, Chief of Clan Chattan in a manuscript history of the Gordons, who wore (*c.* 1572) a 'yellow war coat', which among his people was 'the badge of the Chieftaines or heads of Clans'.

The *lèine croich* was a very practical piece of clothing that could be lengthened or shortened as required by letting down or taking up the excess linen kept fastened at the waist by a belt. It was something of a knapsack too, and food and valuables could be lodged in its huge sleeves. Lesley writes of the saffron shirt's 'numerous folds and wide sleeves', which 'flowed abroad loosely to the knees', and this abundance of cloth may well have had a protective element, perhaps even enough to absorb a sword blow. Indeed, Martin says a mighty twenty-four 'ells' of cloth (one ell is 95 cm) were used to make it – he also reckons the war-coat to have been given up at the end of the sixteenth century. Until then, it was just as commonly worn in Ireland (Henry VIII tried to ban 'any shirt ... dyed with saffron'). William Camden in his *Annals* (1615) talks of galloglass in the time of Elizabeth I parading in 'yellow shirts dyed with saffron', just as Derricke notes of the shirts worn by Irish 'kern':

> Their shirtes be verie straunge,
> Not reaching paste the thigh,
> With pleates on pleates they pleated are,
> As thicke as pleates may lye.

The face of Gaelic warfare: a cattle raid from Derricke's Image of Irelande. *All the raiders wear saffron shirts and carry long dirks, as used by both Gaelic Scots and Irish. The raid begins as a 'packe of prowling mates' appear out of the woods (marked by Derricke 'A'). Next they loot and plunder a farmstead ('B'), before ('C') they 'returne back to the wood'. (University of Edinburgh)*

Gaelic helmets of the fifteenth and sixteenth centuries from art and tomb sculpture of the day.

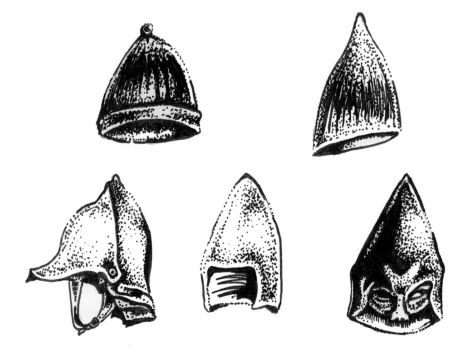

SHIELDS

No Scottish shields (*sgiath* in Gaelic) of medieval date survive, but the leather and wood 'targe' (*targaid*), as used in the seventeenth and eighteenth centuries, evidently already existed. Targes are specifically referred to by the Scots Parliament in 1456 and 1481. On the latter occasion, parliament orders that axemen without spears or bows are to have 'a targe of tree or led[er]' with two arm-straps, based on an example sent to every shire. Jean de Beaugué, a French soldier who fought at the siege of Haddington (1548–9), thus describes the shields of the Scots as 'targets', as does the English *Trewe Encountre*, written shortly after Flodden. The heavy wooden 'pavise' was the best protection against arrows, and according to Edward Hall's *Triumphant Reigne of Kyng Henry VIII*, these were carried by Scots (probably those in the front rank) at Flodden. Conventional heater-shaped shields are depicted on tombs and in the Carlisle Charter, while what may be a 'buckler' appears on a fifteenth-century grave-slab at Kcills, Knapdale. Some Scots carried rectangular shields at Pinkie, estimated by Patten to be 'about a foot in breadth and half a yard in length', with handles 'made very cunningly of two cord lengths.'

'BOW AND AX, KNYF AND SWERD'

The ordinary Highlander was the least encumbered of all Scots fighters. Here was the dreaded Highland *ceathairne* or 'caterans,' fearsome figures who John of Fordun (d. after 1384) calls 'wild and untamed, rough and unbending ... comely in form but unsightly in dress.' A literal translation of *ceathairne* is 'peasantry,' but in this context it refers to a stratum of free farmers and countrymen who collectively formed the sword-arm of a *clann* (Gaelic: 'children').

Major observes of rank-and-file Cameron and Chattan clansmen that 'their possessions are few, but they follow one chief as leader of the family'. When a chief sent out word to muster, hundreds of 'relatives' (both real and imagined) would gather, bristling with arms. A view of Highland weaponry around 1420 is given by Andrew Wyntoun, Prior of Lochleven, in his account of a judicial combat between two Highland clans at the North Inch of Perth in the presence of Robert III (reigned 1390–1406):

> At Sanct Johnestone besid the Freris
> All thai entrit in Barreris
> Wyth Bow and Ax, Knyf and Swerd
> To deil amang thaim thar last werd.

Bower writes of the same event that the combatants were 'armed only with swords, bows and arrows and without mantles or other armour except axes'. Wyntoun's mention of 'Knyf' is echoed by Major a century later in a clear reference to the dirk or 'a strong dagger, single edged but of the sharpest', a weapon Highlanders 'always carry'. The Gaelic *sgian* for knife is anglicised to 'skeine' by Dymmok when he states it to be a standard side-arm of the galloglass. Daggers 'scharp onlie at the on syde' are also mentioned by Pitscottie in his own broad-brush portrait of Highlanders, confirming that this was a universally carried tool, even if the actual term 'dirk' does not appear to have been used much before 1557, when Mans McGillmichell was charged with assaulting Andrew Dempster around Inverness with 'ane dowrk.'

SCOTTISH SWORDS

The typical medieval Scottish sword (Gaelic: *claidheamh*) was a flat-bladed chopping weapon, even after thin, thrusting types became popular elsewhere in Europe. As late as Pinkie, the Scots still had swords which Patten describes as 'all notably broad ... and universally so made to slice'. Early Scottish swords had lobated pommels (divided into separate pods or 'lobes') similar to those used by the Vikings, but from the fourteenth or fifteenth century the fashion became large disc-like pommels, with drooping quillons (the arms of the sword's cross-guard) and langets (strips of metal fixed to the head of a weapon to give added strength) protruding on to the blade. At the start of the sixteenth century the awesome Highland two-handed sword appeared, a weapon more recently called *claidheamh-mór*, Gaelic for 'great sword.' The anglicised version of the word, 'claymore', was first used in the seventeenth century but at that time meant a basket-hilted broadsword. Only later did 'claymore' come to mean a two-handed sword. The defining characteristic of the Highland two-handed sword

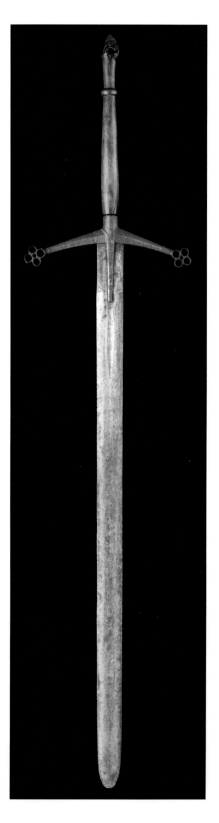

Visualising the Gaelic world at war, c. 1500. At left and centre are two Highland gentlemen. The right-hand figure is an Irish 'kern' carrying sword and targe – his attire is identical to that of the typical Scots 'cateran'. (Photo by Andrew Hayes)

Single-handed Scottish sword, c. 1400–50. This elegant weapon has the distinctive Scots traits of a hilt with down-swept quillons terminating in globules, and a heavy wheel pommel. (The Trustees of the National Museums of Scotland)

was its openwork quatrefoil terminals (reminiscent of early Christian stone crosses in Scotland), each pierced with four holes, on downward-sloping, gently tapering quillons.

Two-handed Highland swords are normally between 1.3 and 1.4 metres long and weigh around 2.5 kg, making them smaller than continental European two-handed swords, although their blades are usually German. Despite many references to their use, few Highland two-handed swords survive – perhaps only thirty that have not been significantly modified – and it is likely that they were the preserve of the *duine-uasal* class, their closest henchmen, champions and clan executioners. That being so, Scottish swords were usually big, often big enough to be wielded two-handed. Lowlanders called this compromise 'halflang' ('hand and a half'). Pitscottie thus describes Lachlan MacLean of Duart's 'schoisin men' as making their way to Flodden with 'bowis and halfen [halflang] and haberschownis of mailze' – as a group, 'halflang' captured the general look of their broad-bladed swords, whether single- or double-handed.

German blades were also imported to make single-handed swords in Scotland, as they were for a two-handed type that emerged in the Lowlands around the same time as the Highland two-hander. The Lowland two-handed sword is generally larger than its Highland equivalent (but usually less well finished), and is distinguished by thin quillons set at a near-right angle to the blade, and sharply downward-turned terminals.

TWO-HANDED SWORDS: THE TEST OF BATTLE

A little over a month after Flodden, the Scottish government announced that for 'the defence of the bordouris' all the king's lieges were to 'reforme thar harness and abilzementis for war and mak thame fensable wapinnis sic as speris, Leitht axis, and Jedwart stavis, halbertis, and gud twa handit swordis'. In other words, lairds were to make sure that at least some of their followers were armed with two-handed weapons, including decent two-handed swords. This announcement came in the aftermath of a defeat in which the king and eight to ten thousand of his subjects perished. One small victory had been won by the several thousand Highlanders commanded by Alexander Gordon, Earl of Huntly (d. 1524). They had careered into a brigade of Cheshire and Lancashire men, and Pitscottie graphically recounts how 'Hunttleis Hieland men witht their bowis and tua handit swords wrocht [worked] sa manfullie that they defait the Inglischmen bot ony slaughter on their syde.' Then, as Pitscottie marvellously puts it, Huntly and his officers 'blew thair trumpattis and convenit thair men agane to thair standartis.' In the days and weeks after Flodden, there must have been a realisation among Scottish commanders that two-handed swords (still a fairly new weapon in Scotland) suited – like the axe – the swift, attacking tactics of their men. Besides which, it was one of the few weapons capable of felling the sturdy armoured knights and yeomen of England.

AXES

Yet even after the advent of two-handed swords, the battle-axe (in Gaelic, *tuagh* means 'axe' and *tuagh-chatha* means 'battle-axe') remained a favourite weapon for the Scots. Axes had long been closely associated with the Scottish fighting technique. Froissart for one was struck by the size of the Scots' axes, so large they had to be carried on the shoulder, with which 'they deal some very hard blows.' In John Barbour's *Brus* (c. 1375–7), King Robert delivers 'the first stroke of the fight' at Bannockburn in 1314 by killing Sir Henry de Bohun with a single blow of his axe. Froissart records that at Otterburn James, Earl of Douglas (c.1358–88), 'saw that his men were falling back, so, to recover the lost ground and show his warlike qualities, he took a two-handed axe and plunged into the thickest of the fight.'

FAR LEFT
Highland two-handed sword, early sixteenth century; the iron hilt has wooden grips covered in leather, and the blade is steel.

LEFT
A fine example of a Lowland two-handed sword, c.1550. The Scottish hilt (perhaps Edinburgh or Stirling) is of iron (grips missing), with a steel blade, probably German. (Peter Finer Antique Arms and Armour)

Even so, it was the galloglass who became synonymous with the axe. St Leger and Dymmok call their axe a 'sparre': the very word was a shorthand for the soldier himself, Dymmok stating 'eighty of which sparres make a battle of galloglass.' The galloglass axe was a particular type, and a number of axe-heads survive in Ireland that match contemporary descriptions and visual depictions. Arranged chronologically, they reveal a developing type from an elegantly curved axe-head of Norse origin, through to a sharply angled blade likened by Dymmok to a halberd, and by St Leger to 'the axe of the Towre'.

It is, however, possible that some of the axes referred to by Bower and Wyntoun as weapons used by Highlanders are of a sort known as 'Lochaber axes'. This was a type of glaive or halberd, and is first mentioned in 1501 when James IV ordered 'ane batale ax maid of Lochabirt fasoun'. Only the staves actually came from Lochaber, then a thickly wooded area. This is certainly the weapon Major has in mind when he speaks of Highlanders being typically armed with 'a small halbert' – a weapon he claims was in use at Bannockburn. The 'Lochaber axe', he informs us, 'is employed by the wild Scots of the north', and is distinguished from other pole-arms by being 'single-edged only.'

The advantage of the Lochaber was its long cutting edge, which could slice through the thick layers of plaiding that most Gaels wore. Its hook was also useful, not only for pulling men from their horses, but for ripping clothing apart and pulling opponents to the ground. A similar weapon evolved in the Borders during the same period called the 'Jedburgh Staff', so-named because it was made by the smiths of that town, who, Major explains, 'fasten a piece of iron four feet long to the end of a

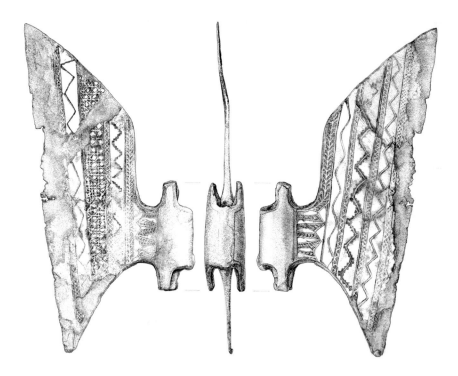

Axe-head, made from a single piece of folded iron, overlaid with decoration in silver foil. Sixteenth century, from Clonteevy, Co. Tyrone, now in the Ulster Museum. Almost certainly the weapon of a galloglass, perhaps a captain or constable of galloglass. Drawing by Dierdre Crone. (After C. Bourke, 2001)

stout staff.' Major makes mention too of the 'double-axe of Leith', again portraying it as a weapon used at Bannockburn. This was probably the Scottish equivalent of the English bill, because Major calls it 'a piece of iron formed hook-wise at the end of a stout staff – this serves as a bill-hook or axe; this most serviceable weapon is in use among the English yeomen.'

PROJECTILE WEAPONS

The bow (*bogha* in Gaelic) was carried by most Highlanders, both high- and low-born, but was much less used by Lowlanders. Pitscottie refers to Highlanders armed with 'bowis and dartes'; Major too presents the bow as a common Highland weapon. Lughaidh O'Clery, meanwhile, says Hebrideans fighting for Red Hugh O'Donnell against Elizabeth I in 1594 had bows strung 'with long twanging hempen strings', which fired 'sharp pointed arrows that whizzed in their flight.' The bow and the javelin (Gaelic: *gath*) were also an efficient means of catching dinner – an important consideration for soldiers without much logistical support. Perhaps this is evident in Buchannan's observation that Highlanders fire arrows 'for the most part hooked, with a barble on either side, which once entered within the body, cannot be drawne forth againe, unless the wounde be made wider.' These sound like barbed hunting arrowheads pressed into battlefield use – John Taylor in his *Pennylesse Pilgrimage* (1618) in fact says of Highlanders that 'their weapons are long bowes and forked arrows ... with these armes I found many of them armed for the hunting.'

Hunting arrows could, of course, be used in battle if there was nothing else to hand, but they would be ineffective against armoured men, since the purpose of the barbs is

to make a large surface wound so that an animal running from a huntsman will, in theory, bleed to death. A straight 'bodkin' warhead would be a better choice if the target were wearing armour, as this makes a single, deep puncture. The use of hunting arrows in a military context (and a bundle of hunting arrows is carried by one Irish warrior in Dürer's drawing of 1521) would be because the average Highlander had no other choice. He could only improvise and adapt what he had to hand from his ordinary life as a cattle farmer (or thief!) and huntsman.

De Beaugué refers to the 'large bows' of the Highlanders, but Scottish bows (see the Carlisle Charter for their size) were certainly smaller than the mighty English longbow. The Gaelic bow in particular was a stalker's weapon; given its size and that it was drawn only to the chest rather than ear, it would be logical to think that it was also less powerful than the English war-bow. Count John de Perilhos, a Catalan in Ireland in 1397, claims otherwise, asserting that the archers of Níall Óg, King of Tír Eoghain, had bows 'as short as half a bow of England, but they shoot as far as the English ones'; unless re-curved they cannot have offered much punch against armour. Besides, Froissart is adamant that 'the Scots do not much trouble with the bow' because 'in battle they approach at once'. The Highland bow must be seen as a skirmishing weapon, and while further archers were recruited from Ettrick in the Borders, bowmen were not deployed *en masse* by the Scots as they were by the English.

Projectile siege engines such as the trebuchet (see the Carlisle Charter) were also used by the Scots, though poorly. The same was true of gunpowder weapons in the 1500s, for despite Scottish fascination for these new toys, guns were used with almost no skill at Flodden, Solway Moss (1542) and Pinkie. Borderers opted, until firearms became common, for a small, hand-wound crossbow called a 'latch' that could be fired from the saddle – again, better for skirmishing than massed volleys.

SPEARS

The real strength of medieval Scottish armies lay in infantry attacking with two-handed weapons, and attacking or defending with spears. A spear (Gaelic: *sleagh*) of about 8 feet was normal in the Highlands. In the Lowlands it was a 12-foot implement, and the image of a spear-armed Lowlander in a jack can be accepted as an accurate caricature, just as the Highlander in mail or quilted armour and armed with a two-handed weapon can be. We therefore find Pitscottie able to split the army raised by James V in 1542 into two neat halves: 'XXm in jak and speir' and 'XXm haberjouns and tua handit suordis.'

In battle, Scottish spearmen drew together into the *schiltron*, a tight defensive formation, which, at Stirling Bridge (1297) under the inspired command of Sir William Wallace (d. 1305) and Andrew Murray (d. 1297), defeated the knights of Edward I of England. The Bruce brilliantly developed the *schiltron* into a dynamic, attacking formation and won an even greater victory at Bannockburn. *Vita Edwardi Secundi*, a contemporary English chronicle of events, says the Scots at Bannockburn 'advanced like a thick-set hedge' armed with spears and axes. The likewise

Galloglass in basinets, mail and quilted armour on the tomb of Felim O'Connor, late 1400s, Roscommon abbey, Republic of Ireland (Photographic Unit, Department of Environmental Heritage and Local Government, Ireland).

contemporaneous English *Lanercost Chronicle* likens the charge of the English cavalry into the *schiltrons* at Bannockburn to entering 'a dense forest', which rang to 'a great and terrible crash of spears broken and of destriers wounded to death.'

In an account of the battle of Baugé, fought in western France in 1421, the Scottish author of the mid-fifteenth-century *Book of Pluscarden* describes his compatriots as 'most mighty men at a sudden chase and very good with the spear'. Here some 6,000 Scots serving in France under the Earl of Buchan ripped apart an English army, assailing them, writes *Pluscarden's* author, 'chiefly with spears and maces of iron and lead and keen edged swords'. At Flodden this tried and tested tactic was bastardised to resemble the pike columns of the Swiss and *Landsknechts*, the old 12-foot spear having been abolished by law in 1471 in favour of a pike upwards of 18 feet – with dire results. The unwieldy pike was a poor weapon against the 8-foot English bill, and it was those bills, concludes the *Trewe Encountre*, that 'did beat and hew thaim downe' at Flodden.

Effigy of a warrior armed with spear and sword, Kilmartin Parish Church, Argyll, fourteenth or fifteenth century. (Crown copyright: Royal Commission on the Ancient and Historical Monuments of Scotland)

THE SCOTTISH KNIGHT AND REIVER

Writing in 1551–2, the French ecclesiastic Étienne Perlin assessed the Scottish nobility as 'not so well armed as the French, for they have very little well-made, clean, and polished armour, but use jackets of mail' – as for horses, they 'have the custom of using little ambling nags'. Perlin was right: native Scottish horses were unsuitable for battlefield use, and most Scots knights dismounted to fight. At Northallerton, David had many knights but 'almost all' of them, says Richard, Prior of Hexham (from *c.* 1141), fought on foot, including David himself. Wallace and Murray had only 200 or so cavalry but something like 6,000 infantry at Stirling; Sir Robert Keith commanded no more than 500 cavalrymen at Bannockburn out of an army of perhaps 7,000; James IV's entire army fought on foot at Flodden. The ratio altered dramatically at Ancrum Moor in 1545 when Sir Walter Scott of Buccleuch and the Master of Rothes led about 1,500 Fife 'lances' and Border 'reivers' in an army roughly 2,500-strong, but few, if any, would have been heavy cavalry.

On foot or horseback, the Scottish knight, often of mixed Gaelic-Norman ancestry (like Bruce), was a force to be reckoned with. At Baugé, Sir Robert Stewart of Railston and Sir Hugh Kennedy halted the advance of the entire English army with only a few men. Knights were the only men in Scotland, aside from a few of the

The tomb in Dunkeld cathedral of Alexander Stewart, Earl of Buchan (died c. 1406), alias the 'Wolf of Badenoch.' The illegitimate son of King Robert II, Alexander was a notorious warlord and womaniser. His tomb – one of only a few medieval royal Scottish monuments to survive – shows him clad in full plate armour, though mail is worn for additional defence and to guard vulnerable points requiring flexibility such as the armpits and groin. His helmet is of basinet form, with an added lower face plate, giving excellent protection but reducing freedom of movement. (Crown copyright: Royal Commission on the Ancient and Historical Monuments of Scotland).

most powerful chiefs, who wore full suits of armour. James II (reigned 1437–60) had a German armour sent to him; James IV and James V bought suits of armour from France, and France had earlier supplied armour intended to negate the power of the longbow at Homildon Hill. It did nothing of the sort, but the Scots did not learn their lesson and James IV's noblemen at Flodden were probably even more heavily armoured. As before, heavy armour failed to give them the edge they hoped for. Consequently, the period after Flodden saw a general return among the lesser and middling nobility to mail, brigandines and fabric forms of armour, even if the greatest of magnates, such as the Earl of Huntly, seen encased in a suit of enamel and gilt armour at Pinkie, still provided glamorous figureheads to an army.

A fortunate few did own war-horses, and the antiquarian John Stow (1525–1605) records that on St George's Day 1395 there was 'a great jousting on London Bridge, betwixt David Earl of Crawford of Scotland, and the Lord Wells of England.' 'Lord Wells', Stow is gracious enough to admit, 'was at the third course borne out of the saddle'. Most had only stocky little ponies and, dressed in their light armour, the Scots made better 'hobelars' or mounted infantry. At Myton, Douglas and Thomas Randolph, Earl of Moray (d. 1332) swept aside the men of Yorkshire with a picked force of these dragoon-like soldiers. Scott's tough Border reivers operated in the same way at Ancrum Moor many years later, with their jacks, 'steel bonnets', crossbows, swords and 8-foot lances. Ancrum Moor was no great victory for the Scots, but the guile of Scott and his Borderers trapped the English in a murderous scrum, a place of horror in which only men conditioned by years of war could hope to survive.

Seal of Alexander I (reigned 1107–24). Alexander is represented as a Norman mail-clad lancer mounted on charger – in reality a rare sight in any Scots army. (John Wesley's House and the Museum of Methodism)

Chapter Three

GAELIC BLACKSMITHS AND MEN OF ART

FEW NON-GAELIC speakers will recognise the significance in a name like Gowan, Gow or MacGowan, or in placenames like Balgown on Skye, Ballygown on Mull or Tirrygowan in Aberdeenshire. MacGowan, or *Mac a' Ghobhainn* in its true form, means 'son of the smith' from *gobha* for 'smith' (compare with the Irish *gobae/gabha*, Cornish and Welsh *gof*, and Breton *gov*). Unlike his modern counterpart, the blacksmith in the classical Gaelic vein was a respected professional, indeed a gentleman, often working on a hereditary basis and establishing minor dynasties of metalworkers which sometimes lasted for many generations – and it was these men who made armour and weapons in the Highlands.

More often than not, we know more about the armourer-smiths as men than we do about their activities as craftsmen. Our main source for their lives are the songs, stories and

Key to map:

A. *Morrison of Rodel, Harris*
B. *MacLeod of Suardal, Skye*
C. *MacRury of Balgown, Skye*
D. *Robert A' Phetie of Loch Shiel*
E. *MacEachern of Morven*
F. *MacEachern of Islay*
G. *MacEachern of Craignish*
H. *MacPhederan of Benderloch*
I. *Macnab of Barachastlain*
J. *McCaillirin of Icrachan*
K. *Fletcher of Glenlyon*
L. *MacFarlane of Innerwick*
M. *Finlay of Killin*
N. *MacRury of North Uist*
O. *MacRury of Benbecula*
P. *MacRury of South Uist*
Q. *MacInnes of Mull*

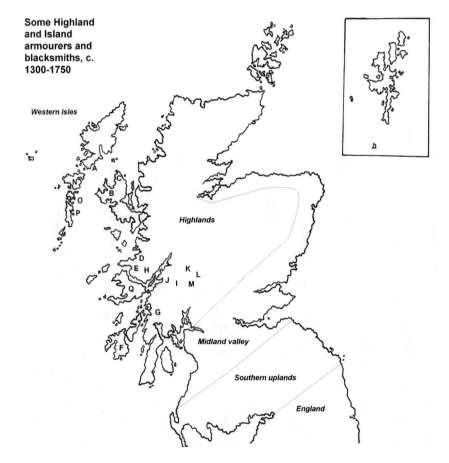

Some Highland and Island armourers and blacksmiths, c. 1300-1750

Western Isles

Highlands

Midland valley

Southern uplands

England

verse of Gaelic Scotland, some of which were written down by Georgian and Victorian travellers while the oral tradition was still alive in the Highlands. The pre-Culloden, pre-Clearance Highlands were a place where change came only very slowly, a society which was so deeply conservative that the usual historical boundary marks of 'medieval', 'early modern' and even 'modern' are almost meaningless. Gaelic smiths did not keep written records of their work, nor did they sign the arms and armour they made, presumably because they did not expect their clientele to include outsiders to the local community. This truly was society at its most basic, tribal state of development, and yet it was one capable of producing superbly crafted metalwork, albeit with a deadly, warlike purpose.

WORKERS IN IRON

A story survives that one Highland chief, told that his smith must die, offered two women in exchange for the smith's life. The armourer or blacksmith of the Highlands received such favour because his skills were rare and because Gaelic society had a great respect for master craftsmanship. No community could survive for long without a smith, and from a chief's perspective a smith who could make weapons and armour was a source of power. In the Gaelic world, it was thought right and proper for a son to follow the trade or profession of his father. This not only made practical sense in an isolated, rural community, but it also conformed to an arcane and patri-lineal system of society devised by the ancient Celts. An eighth-century Irish tract on the laws of status is so precise as to rank the blacksmith as belonging to the *aire déso*, the lowest level of nobility. The same document grants membership of this social bracket to the poet (*file*), bard-historian (*seanchaidh*), lawgiver (*brithem*), physician (*ligiche*), and master mason and carpenter (*saer*), the smith being specifically rated on a par with the physician. Together, these skilled and learned people comprised a hereditary caste known as the *oes dàna* or 'men of art.' This was a term coined in Ireland in the early centuries AD, following an idea that had existed among the Gauls since at least the first century BC. It was a system that was to survive in Scotland until Culloden, and in some instances into the modern age.

DISTRICT AND CLAN

The Highland *gobha* was a man who worked primarily with iron, as opposed to the *ceàrd* who worked with precious metals and copper alloy (it was also the term for a potter). Iron (*iarann*) and steel were not rigidly defined, and ferrous metals were all referred to as 'iron'; the Gaelic *cruaidh* for steel really only means 'hard'. Within the realms of base metals the Gaelic blacksmith ranged free. As both an armourer and all-round blacksmith, he was a generalist rather than a specialist, capable of running a cottage armaments industry while patching up cooking pots, forging farm tools and acting as a farrier. He made what was asked of him by his clan or local community. Some armourer-smiths certainly had their own specialities, such as the Fletchers (Mac-an-leistear, 'children of the man of arrows') of Glenlyon, hereditary bowyers and arrow-makers to the MacGregors, a warlike paymaster if ever there was one. The MacInnes of Mull acted as the same to MacKinnon of MacKinnon, and the bowyer-fletcher, and from the seventeenth century the gunsmith, were probably the only real specialist armourers to be found within the Scottish Gael.

At any rate, having a particular specialism did not stop an armourer from taking on other work, and we therefore find Macnab of Barachastlain, Glenorchy, one of the last of the traditional Gaelic smiths, described by a neighbour at the end of the eighteenth century as an eclectic polymath – 'at once a lock-smith, blacksmith, armourer, and ironmonger, which renders him very useful, and very much esteemed.' From the fifteenth to the nineteenth century the Macnabs crafted coats of mail, helmets, swords, targes, dirks and pistols, specimens of which were shown by two Macnab brothers with 'triumph' to the Roxburghshire poet and linguist Dr John Leyden (1775–1811), who notes that their treasured ancestral relics 'could hardly have been more rusty had they been buried with them.'

The Macnabs are said by some to have been jewellers too. Yet gold is, the Irish saying goes, broken with iron, and it was this military craft that did most for the smith's prestige – so much so that it exempted them from the tribal-feudal obligations of military service expected of other clansmen. A smith who could not make armour or weapons was no use to a Highland chief, for Highland society at its heart was warlike, militarised and prone to violence. Consequently, many of the great smithing families are remembered first and foremost as armourers to chiefs, who bestowed land on them in return for their metalworking skills: the MacLeods of Suardal as armourers to MacLeod of MacLeod; the MacRurys of *Baile Ghobhain* (Balgown, 'Township of the Smith'), Skye, as armourers to MacDonald of Sleat; the Fletchers of Glenlyon as bowyers to MacGregor of MacGregor; and the Macnabs of Barachastlain, are to this day styled 'ancient Armourers and Standard Bearers' to Macnab of Macnab.

Some families are commemorated in oral tradition, song and verse as specifically swordsmiths – craftsmen like the MacPhederans of Benderloch, a late medieval

Barachastlain today, home to the Macnabs from 1440 until 1823 when the settlement passed to the McNicol family. Kate Macnab, 'spinster, crofter', was still living at Barachastlain with the McNicols in 1892–3.

family of armourers associated with the Campbells whose workshop was near the present Barcaldine House, Ferlochan, Argyll. In the eyes of the bards, the sword was the most aristocratic and expensive of all weapons; it was the weapon of heroes. It was inevitable, then, that Gaelic storytellers would often focus on a blacksmith's swordsmithing skills, since this is the weapon smiths supply to the heroes in their tales. The claim is made in an old tale that Duncan Macnab of Barachastlain made swords for the King of Scots in the fifteenth century, which may or may not be true. However, as in the Lowlands, Highland smiths usually bought German sword blades rather than forging their own, which they then put together with a hilt, grips and scabbard made by themselves or other local craftsmen. Even so, Robert A'Phetie, 'Great Smith' to the Clanranald in the following century, is afforded the accolade as a great swordsmith in his district of Moidart (we hear nothing about the mundane, civilian ironwork which he must also have carried out).

We can only guess what else Robert might have made, but without question both he and the Macnabs and others, as smiths to powerful chiefs, would have made whatever arms and equipment was required. The making of mail shirts and hoods – as worn by virtually every Highland nobleman – would unquestionably have formed a large part of their work, as would the making of conical helmets, targes, battle-axes, Lochaber axes, dirks, spears and bows: these, as we have seen, were the foundations of the Highland armoury. There are references to the Macnabs making most of these items, and we can regard their output as typical. As for the

ABOVE LEFT
Grave of Alexander Macnab of Barran and Barachastlain (1747–1814), Glenorchy Parish Kirk, Dalmally. He founded a second smithy and township at Barran while his uncles Malcolm and Donald continued to run Barachastlain.

ABOVE
Francis, 16th Chief of the Macnabs (1734–1816). Francis wears his claymore as he enjoys a dram. His snuff mull, made from a ram's horn, sits upon the table top. The Macnabs of Barachastlain were descended from the chiefly line by a cadet branch begun in the fifteenth century by Duncan, first of the Barachastlain armourers.

MacPhederans, a glimpse of a wider output than swords is contained in a stanza concerning bow-making:

> Bow of the yew of Easragan,
> Feather of the eagle of Loch Treig,
> The yellow wax of Baille-nan-gaillean,
> Arrowhead from the craftsman MacPhederan.

Tanners rather than smiths may have supplied the leather armour needed by the gentry (though the Macnabs made leather-covered targes), but the ordinary cateran would have made his own. The *Book of Clanranald* describes a medieval 'King of the Gael' wearing a 'fine tunic' of satin 'ingeniously woven by ladies and their daughters', beneath his armour and padded jerkin. Perhaps it was the women of the clan (who customarily were weavers) who made the actouns, quilted coats and saffron-shirts for their war-mad menfolk.

IRON ORES IN SCOTLAND

In order to make metal armour and weapons for his chief and clan, the smith needed iron. In his *Dreme of the Realme of Scotland*, Sir David Lindsay (*c.*1490–1555), Lord Lyon King of Arms, speaks of Scotland's wealth of ores: 'Of every mettell we have the rich Minis'. Major states that the Highlanders 'have halberds of great sharpness, for their iron ore is good.' But as has already been noted, a great many surviving Scottish swords have blades that were made in Germany, and so the question immediately presents itself: were any of Scotland's own ores good enough to make arms and armour? Lindsay's picture of Scotland as a land of metallic bounty is utterly

Tom-nan-Gobha or 'Smith's Hillock' near Dalmally. Its use to a blacksmith must have been its good water supply, tumbling down the hillside in the form of several waterfalls.

at odds with the Scots' looting of Furness in 1316, who *Lanercost* states were 'delighted with the abundance of iron which they found there, for Scotland is not rich in iron.' Similarly, Froissart felt nothing was to be had in Scotland 'without great difficulty': everything had to be imported ready-made from Flanders, for there was 'neither iron to shoe horses, nor leather to make harness'.

Froissart exaggerates, but as a general impression of a land deficient in key resources needed for war – iron and hardwoods – it is an accurate one. The geological truth of the matter is that while Scotland has strong deposits of copper, lead and gold, its indigenous iron is largely poor-quality 'bog-iron' (layers of ferrous oxide that have developed in the soil due to the interaction of rain and acid soils). Some bog iron was mined in central and Lowland Scotland from the sixteenth century, but bog iron is far too low in quality to be used to make weapons and armour or objects requiring tensile strength. For these, the higher-grade 'ironstone' (sedimentary rock with a substantial level of iron compounds) must be used. Unfortunately, Scotland has only limited deposits of ironstone, and there is virtually none in the Highlands. There was, apparently, enough to make cannon in Scotland's first blast furnace in the mountains of Wester Ross in 1610, but such enterprises, reflecting the limited availability of ores, were often short-lived. As late as 1719 a spy named Henry Kalmeter working for the Swedish mining business reported that the only ironworks operating in Scotland was a small foundry at Canonbie, near the border with England.

Later still, the famous Bonawe ironworks opened on Loch Etive, Argyll, in 1753. As a site for metalworking the area has much to recommend it. It is thickly wooded with oak, hazel, ash, birch and willow trees, and with a ready water supply, and it is no coincidence that the Bonawe works were built close to the old forge of the McCaillirins of Ichrachan. The McCaillirins were a family of patriotic medieval armourers in Glen Nant who rose to distinction for their arrowheads, it is said, in the time of Wallace – but all the ore 'smelted' at Bonawe, and presumably before that at Ichrachan, was shipped in from mines elsewhere (in the case of Bonawe, bog iron from central Scotland and Cumbria). Nothing was mined locally. It was probably this shortage of good iron that was on the minds of the Highlanders stationed in south-west Scotland in 1678 against Covenanters who, according to a poem by

Grave of Peter Campbell, Highland smith and farrier, Muckairn Parish Kirk, Taynuilt. Campbell is buried close to the site of the McCaillirns of Ichrachan's forge, who later took the name of Campbell. The later Bonawe smelting works were built in the same area.

Lieutentant Colonel William Cleland (published 1697), 'pull the locks' from doors and 'takes away our Iron in laids'.

Though educated men, Lindsay and Major's sense of the metals found in Scotland was based more on hearsay than knowledge of actual mining activity in their country. Like the English in Ireland, there was a certain kind of 'Renaissance' urban Scot who was preoccupied with the idea that the mountains on the horizon were places of hidden, untapped mineral wealth, a richness ineffectively exploited by the lazy savages occupying those tracts of wilderness. They were completely wrong, and, as in Ireland, the iron for crafting arms and armour almost always had to be imported from abroad. Danzig and Stockholm, which traded with Scotland from at least the fourteenth century, were a vital source and both made regular shipments of good-quality iron and hardwoods to Dundee and other ports.

WORKING PRACTICES

The Highlands were not an easy environment to work in, and armourers were faced by the second, though less serious obstacle of a lack of top quality fuels for smelting. Smelting is the removal of slag impurities from ore by heating, and is the first stage in smithing. Before the use of coal, charcoal burnt in an anaerobic environment within a bloomery furnace was the best heat source for smelting. The demand placed

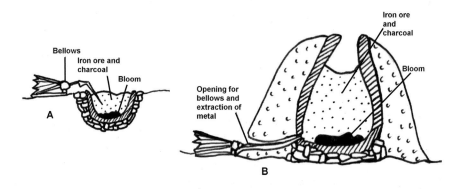

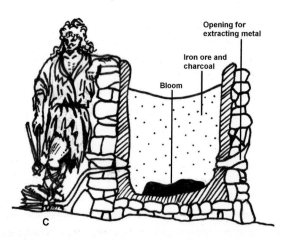

The development of the bloomery, from simple bowl furnace dug into the ground (a), to above ground bloomery (b), to large, free-standing structure (c).

A view of Barachastlain in its medieval heyday.

on woodland was terrific: at the Bonawe works in the eighteenth and nineteenth centuries, 10,000 acres of woodland were needed to make 700 tons of pig iron. Woodland had to be carefully managed, and a charter survives dated 1632 in which Sir Colin Campbell of Glenorchy grants the armourer-smith Patrick 'Gow' Macnab (*c.* 1600–81) 'the two merkland of Barrechastellan' so long as, among other stipulations, he agrees 'to keep the woods undestroyed'.

The McCaillirins were fortunate to have their forge in an area of deciduous woodland, but pines are more common in the Highlands. Though quick growing, pines cannot be coppiced and create a lower temperature when burnt than hardwoods. This lack of heat would produce only small quantities of useable pig iron from raw ore. To get round this obstacle, most Highland smiths must have had ready-made, pre-smelted iron bars or 'billets' delivered to their forges (even in the Middle Ages intrepid merchants and tinkers ventured up to the Highlands). After smelting (or upon arrival of pre-smelted billets) came 'bloomsmithing' as the smith refined the masses of iron (or 'blooms') by repeated hammering and heating. Strengthening would then take place by further heating, beating and quenching until the metal became a useable shape.

Gaelic songs and stories give vivid snap-shots of conditions in the 'smiddy', and make clear that the tools and working environment of the Highland armourer-smith would be recognisable to any modern blacksmith. The basic tools of the forge, then as now, were anvil (in Gaelic *innean*), hammer (*ord*), tongs (*teanchair*), and hearth (*teinntein*). Tools are the focus of the Irish story of the sons of Eochaid Muigmedóin,

The ruins of Barachastlain show the buildings to have been a mix of drystone and mortared construction. In places, the walls are a metre thick – sturdy enough for one of the houses to be inhabited until 1953.

in which Eochaid's sons are tested by having to rescue the contents of a burning forge. The item each son takes reveals his inner man:

> Brian carried out the hammers on his back, Ailill carried out the weaponry, Fiachna
> carried out the water-trough, Fergus carried out the bundles of well-dried firewood.
>   The bellows, the hammers – stout the strength – the block on which the anvil
> stood, aye and the anvil itself, Níall the noble-modest saved.

THE SMITH AS WIZARD

In early Gaelic saga, we find a comparable figure to the Germanic Weland, the Roman Vulcan and the Greek Hephaistos. The wizard-blacksmith was a well-developed character in Gaelic lay and legend, and Highlanders would be familiar with such characters as Sithcenn 'smith of Tara who was a man learned in occult arts and a prophet of note'; or Olc Aiche 'the druid smith', who when his grandson was born, 'put five protective circles about him, against wounding, against drowning, against enchantment, against wolves, that is to say, against every evil.' This was the essential reputation of the smith in pre-Christian days. After the spread of Christianity, the smith's powers waned, but something of the supernatural lingered about his forge and, most of all, in his tools. That the smith could transform lumps of ore into useful objects made him a miracle worker to the local folk. To clerical eyes, an element of pagan magic still surrounded the smith, even after two smiths, Eloi (*c.* 590–*c.* 660, patron saint of metalworkers in general) and

A blacksmith in a sixteenth-century Flemish woodcut.

Dunstan (*c*. 900–*c*. 988, patron saint of armourers and locksmiths, jewellers and goldsmiths), were elevated to sainthood.

The smith was commonly believed to be a healer who was able to ward off evil spirits and make charms – such objects as the girdle of mail armour ensuring safe childbirth that can be seen in the National Museum of Ireland. Martin tells of a smith of the Isles, thirteenth of his line, who had inherited the gift of being able to cure illness by placing a patient on his anvil and coming at him with a 'big hammer in both his hands, and making his Face all Grimace' – bringing his hammer to a halt just above the patient's face. Martin assures the reader that the smith had a 'dexterity of Managing the Hammer with Descretion', and the folk of the area swore by this treatment for many ailments.

Smiths sometimes used their powers to kill, usually by making weapons of invincible power, such as the 'Rough grey iron of wizardry they had mounted on poles' that confronts the legendary Fionn Mac Cumhal in *Duanaire Finn*: 'giddiness and faint sickness came over Fionn and Fian at the sight of them.' MacEachern of Crossbrig's son was said to have learned magical swordsmithing after he was abducted by fairies. His father, armed with a dirk, cockerel and Bible, rescued him – but fairy magic had rubbed off on the lad, who thereafter was able to make swords 'the like of which was never seen in the country before.' Given such perceived powers – powers with anything but a Christian source – it is hardly surprising that the *Faed Fiada*, a prayer attributed to St Patrick, should contain the exhortation: 'I summon today all these virtues ... against spells of women, smiths and druids.'

The 'Clanranald anvil'

The so-called 'Clanranald anvil' is an important record of the Gaelic smith. This enigmatic block of iron gets its name on the basis that it was found a century ago in the deserted township of Upper Mingarry on the Moidart Peninsula. The local priest then gave it to the West Highland Museum at Fort William. Moidart was a homeland of the MacDonalds of Clanranald, a powerful clan named after Ranald, third son of John, First Lord of the Isles, who in about 1370 was granted by his father the lordship of Garmoran, which included Moidart. Nothing more of the anvil's provenance is known. But if we are to believe an eighth-century Irish proverb that 'Any anvil which is struck teaches he who strikes it; it is not taught', we may still find it has secrets to reveal.

There has never been a standard type of anvil, but the most famous variety is the flat-topped anvil used by the general blacksmith and farrier with a beak-shaped 'horn' protruding horizontally, and a flat rectangular 'face' or top surface. The Clanranald example belongs to a hornless, squarish style of anvil popular with blacksmiths and armourers throughout Europe from about the mid fifteenth to the mid seventeenth century. The Clanranald example is small (as this type of anvil often is), though very heavy: approximately 20 cm high with a working surface of about 17 cm in diameter. The face of hornless anvils is usually flat, with curved depressions and creases for making particular shapes restricted to the sides.

The Clanranald anvil is unusual in that its face is also covered with angled ridges. This varied surface would have provided most of the curves, ridges, grooves, half-ovals and half-rectangles a smith needed. The Clanranald anvil is clearly something of a 'multi-tool' on which a wide range of objects could be made (not just armour). It would suit a smith expecting a wide range of commissions, or perhaps an itinerant smith, the latter having been a common figure in Celtic Britain, and one who in Ireland survived into modern times as the inimitable tinker. Once the block was steadied and given spring by a wooden stump (Gaelic: *ceap* or *ploc*) a smith could turn out helmets, breastplates, greaves for the shins, vambraces for the arms, as well as make repairs to other pieces of armour, on its cleverly designed surface.

We may want to question whether 'anvil' (from the Old English *anfilte* for 'beat'), an implement generally defined as having a flat surface on which hard hammering and grinding can be performed, is the best term to be applied here.

Three views of the 'Clanranald anvil,' showing the large semicircular wing protruding from its side and its surface pock-marked with hammer blows. (West Highland Museum, Fort William)

Woodcut of a blacksmith and his anvil from William Caxton's Game and Play of the Chess, *1483.*

The absence of a flat working surface suggests a function closer to a 'swage' (Old French *souage*, 'decorative groove'), the smith's die or block used for the precise shaping of cold sheet metal. Even so, it is undeniably more a general block than a swage. Besides, excessive pedantry over terms, especially if they are not Gaelic, is unhelpful, given that the title 'Clanranald anvil' is an English one, and a modern one at that. That said, it has been beaten as brutally – even destructively – as any anvil over a period of many years, and its surface is scarred with hammer marks. Once crisp edges are now completely gone, rendering the block useless as a tool, which begs the question of why a tool that could no longer be used was not melted down and turned into something else. Anvils and blocks were not considered inherently valuable objects, and early examples do not often survive. This block clearly meant something to someone.

The anvil was a recognised symbol for honour and masculinity in early Irish literature, and phrases such as 'firm anvil of manliness', 'an anvil for supporting the honour of his household' abound, just as 'bold Níall' is described as 'Tara's mighty anvil in the east'. Another potent image comes with Níall Nóigíallach's rescue of an anvil and block from a burning forge, which marks him out as a better choice for king than his brothers. The anvil was, after all, the focal point of the blacksmith's shop, on which the smith gave life to unformed billets. The survival of the Clanranald anvil – whether or not it had any connection with the MacDonalds of Clanranald – must be due to a symbolic or supernatural value it held for the local community.

We first hear of a *Gobha Mór* or 'Great Smith' as resident among the Clanranald in the person of Raibeart A'Pheitidh (Robert A'Phetie) in the sixteenth century. Robert is remembered in Moidart folklore as tacksman of farms on Loch Shiel, probably in the Mingarry area. He is given some tangibility by the riveting tale of his foster son, Donald of the Hammers. Set shortly after Flodden, we learn that Robert's wife Morag acted as nurse to the chief's niece, Mairead, after her marriage to Alasdair an T-Sithchail (Alexander the Peaceful), son of the laird of the Appin Stewarts. One day, a gang of Campbells of Dunstaffnage led by Cailen Uaine (Green Colin) murdered Alasdair and his wife, and seized control of his estate of Invernahyle. Morag had been out walking when the Campbells came, and in her arms she carried Alasdair's only child, Donald.

The Campbells came after Morag, and she hid the baby in a cave with a ball of lard hanging from a string around his neck. Morag was imprisoned for several days by Green Colin. As soon as she was released she ran to the cave, sure that Donald would be dead. But she found him alive, having fed on the ball of lard until it was reduced to the size of a walnut. Morag returned to Moidart where she and her husband raised Donald as their own. At sixteen, Donald was so strong that he could work in the forge with a hammer in each hand, and the local community dubbed him Domhnall nan Ord, 'Donald of the Hammers.'

When Robert and Morag revealed to Donald the truth of his parentage, Donald swore revenge. With a party of warriors, Donald killed Green Colin and nine of his family, before proceeding to attack the Campbells on Loch Awe. Donald moved to Invernahyle, married, had children, and gave his foster-mother a cottage on his lands, presumably because Robert was now dead. Thereafter the records are silent, though local lore says descendants of Clanranald's Great Smith were still living in Ardnamurchan in the early twentieth century.

Gylen Castle on the isle of Kerrera off Oban, built by the MacDougalls in the late sixteenth century. Until falling foul of Robert the Bruce in the fourteenth century, the MacDougalls were amongst the most powerful families in western Scotland. Thereafter many MacDougalls sought their fortune as galloglass in Ireland. The Macnabs took the side of the MacDougalls and were all but ruined in their war with the Bruce – a century later one branch emerges at Barachastlain having reinvented themselves as noted armourers. The theme of lost power is a common one among families following hereditary professions, including armourers, and indeed galloglass.

BLOODLINES

The lives of the Highland armourers really were the stuff of legends, and brimmed with adventure. Throughout the Middle Ages, bloodlines of smiths, sprung from a single common ancestor, spread across the Gàidhealtachd, finding employment among the many clans – each with its own chief who ruled over his people with absolute authority. The MacRurys, based in Trotternish, began as armourer-smiths to the MacDonalds in Skye; around the late seventeenth century a branch moved to North Uist, as others scattered to the Clanranald isles of Benbecula and South Uist. Until the mid 1700s every chief had his smith. Martin, who died in 1718 and was a sometime tutor to the sons of the lairds of Harris and Sleat, describes how chiefs in the Western Isles 'had their fix'd Officers, who were ready to attend them upon all Occasions, whether Military or Civil.' Martin adds that a chief would divide a cow among his officials, 'such as the Physician, Orator, Poet, Bard, Musicians, &c.', giving the head to the smith, as a means of ratifying their 'ancient Leagues of Friendship'. The MacEacherns were another prominent family found working across the west Highlands and islands as armourers and smiths. Those on Islay enjoyed no less a patron than the Lord of the Isles. The various MacEacherns were of one stock and they are described in an early eighteenth-century manuscript history of the Campbells of Craignish as being a notable family in that part of Argyll, besides there being 'other tribes of them yet in Morvine and in Ilay commonly called Clan Gowan, they being haereditary Smiths in these Countries for seaverall Generations.'

Martin says that some chiefs retained their officials on a hereditary basis, whereby they 'continue them from Father to Son ... tho' the Officer had no Charter for the same, but only Custom'. Through wars, famine and every imaginable hardship, the hereditary tradition was almost too strong to break. The MacFarlanes of Innerwick, Perthshire, famous for their swords and daggers, were particularly resilient and continued for no fewer than fourteen generations. So were the MacRurys. Even when after the 'Forty-Five it became almost impossible to make a living as an armourer in the Highlands, the MacRurys would not deviate from their ancestral occupation of working with metal. Malcolm MacRury was still found to be pursuing a living as a blacksmith on North Uist in 1799, and the big-bearded John MacRury (b. 1856/7) was doing the same on the island in the early twentieth century.

The family of John MacRury, blacksmith of An Sruthan Ruadh, North Uist, born on the island in 1856/7. Here MacRury and his wife Catherine (née Stewart) pose with three of their eight daughters. (Comann Eachdraidh Uibhist a' Truath)

FOUNDING FATHERS

The founders of these dynasties of armourers were sometimes near-legendary figures. There is very often more truth than fiction in these tales, and their claims of descent commonly prove genuine, or at least plausible if not verifiable. The MacLeods of Suardal on the Isle of Skye were unusually aristocratic in their origins, being a cadet branch of the chiefly house to whom they were armourers – in their case the mighty MacLeod of MacLeod. The Suardal family claimed descent from John the Savage, sixth Chief of MacLeod (d. *c.* 1442), via the MacLeods of Waternish, and their forge in Glen Suardal was suitably close to the laird's massive pile at Dunvegan. Donald was born around 1715–20 and bore the title *Gobha Shuardail* ('Smith of Suardal'), holding the tacks of Suardal and Duart. The arms of this proud family, suitably enough, includes a Highland two-handed sword.

The Macnabs of Barachastlain were founded by the equally high-born and especially enterprising Duncan, born about 1400–10, the second son of the Chief of the Macnabs. On the death of his father, Duncan set off to northern Italy where he was apprenticed to an armourer. After some years in Italy, Duncan returned home and built a house and forge at Barr á Chaistealain, 'Ridge of the Fort', the site of a prehistoric defensive farmstead above the village of Dalmally, Glenorchy. Today, the ruins can be seen there of three longhouses, three smaller buildings and several agricultural enclosures, made of some massive stone boulders apparently plundered by the Macnabs from the ancient dun.

The Macnabs of Barachastlain had clearly at some point in their history been armourers to their own chief. When this was is unclear. They are referred to by Archibald, 17th Chief of the Macnabs in a letter of 1847 as 'more Anciently The Armourers & Standardbearers of The Chief', though he adds – 'Not having the Ancient Chronological Tables of the Family at hand, I cannot be Particular as to the different dates.' Duncan, at any rate, forged an alliance with the Campbells of Glenorchy, which, as Leyden records, was to last 'for the space of four hundred years', the Macnabs the perpetual 'hereditary smiths of the Breadalbane family' (the Breadalbane family being the Campbells

Armorial stall for Macnab of Barachastlain, Spanish chestnut, chancel of St Conan's Kirk, Loch Awe.

MACNAB · OF · BARCHAISTEALAN

of Glenorchy, ancestors of the Earls of Breadalbane). An early commission for the Macnabs of Barachastlain came from the Glenorchy Campbells, says a very strong oral tradition in Glenorchy – first recorded in the eighteenth century – in 1440 when Duncan was employed to make the ironwork for Kilchurn Castle, until then a ruin on an island on Loch Awe.

The association with the Campbells grew stronger in the seventeenth century, when Duncan's descendant, Patrick 'Gow' received in 1632 the 'tack' of Barachastlain for life in return for his pledge to 'mend all the iron and broken work of the Castle of Glenurquhay [Kilchurn], with the plough irons of Kinchrekan and mill thereof'. As tacksman Patrick held a lease of land from the chief with the right to sub-let for a profit, the standard land-agreement made between a laird and his 'men of art'. Campbell of Glenorchy had other tenants who were blacksmiths, such as the 'Finlay Smyth' who in 1582 paid rent for 'the Smythis markland' at Killin (nearly 50 km east of Barachastlain). Finlay was almost certainly general blacksmith to the community at large, rather than personal smith or armourer to the Laird of Glenorchy. It was Patrick 'Gow' who provided this service during the seventeenth century; from him descends a provable line of Macnab armourer-smiths, all serving the 'Lords of Kilchurn Castle'.

Archibald, 17th Chief of the Macnabs (1778–1860), painted by MacKenzie while Macnab was living in Canada. A copy of this picture hangs in Dundurn Castle, Hamilton, Ontario.

BARDIC SMITHS

More senior than blacksmiths among the 'men of art' were the bards, already prominent in Gaul in the first century BC as living repositories of tribal legend, history and song. But there was, too, a strong bardic note to the identity of the armourer. In the late 1700s, one of the Macnabs of Barachastlain was summarised by his neighbour as 'a kind of bard', meaning not just that he was an enthusiastic poet and singer, but one whose versifying contained pieces of practical instruction and his own, precious metalworking secrets for the next generation. It is no surprise, then, that from a skilled family of armourers and smiths like the Morrisons of Harris sprang an equally accomplished (and virtually illiterate) singer-poet, 'Iain Gobha' or John Morrison of Rodel (1790–1852).

Malcolm Macnab of Barachastlain (1732/3–1823) is a vivid instance of this blending of song and verse with the hard, physical work of the smithy. He was the last of the Macnab Barachastlain armourers, though he was just as bardic, romantic and Gaelic as his ancestors. There is a pleasing story that Malcolm made a *sgian dhu*

ABOVE
Duncan Macnab (1795–1845) is buried in the graveyard of Glenorchy Parish Kirk, Dalmally. He was an ensign at Waterloo and a descendant (probably a grandson) of Malcolm Macnab, last armourer of Barachastlain. Duncan had one daughter, Christina, and a son, John.

ABOVE RIGHT
Grave of Alexander Macnab (1736–1812), merchant in Oban. He was the brother of Malcolm Macnab of Barachastlain, and is buried in Muckairn, Taynuilt. Alexander's great-great-great-grandson Alistair (b. 1937) is the current Representer of Barachastlain.

with a hilt fashioned from the fore leg of a kid for the great Highland balladeer Duncan Bàn MacIntyre. Malcolm would accept no payment from Duncan other than a song praising his skill as a craftsman. Malcolm's own *oeuvre* as a bard appears to be lost apart from a stray ditty concerning Morag, his clumsy maidservant who keeps breaking cooking pots and cutlery. Singing provided rhythm and timing to the smith's work, and the demonic working conditions of the *ceàrdach* or forge – fire, smoke, heat and noise – were a rich seam of metaphor for any bard to mine, as in the *Lay of the Smithy*:

> Daorghlas watched at the workshop,
> 'Tis a certain tale that they fell out;
> He was as red as a coal of the oaktree,
> And his hue like the fruit of the working.

THE END OF AN ERA

As the 1700s wore on the Highland smith was sinking ever lower into social oblivion. From an account by the Parisian naturalist, Professeur Barthélemy Faujas Saint-Fond (1741–1819) we gain a glimpse of Barachastlain in its final days as an armourer's workshop. The well-heeled Frenchman looked around the workshop, 'neither large nor magnificent', and was shown dirks at various stages of production. Macnab (either

Malcolm or his brother Donald) told Saint-Fond that as craftsmen they 'never deviate' from one basic design of dirk because it 'is a very good one, being agreeable to the eye, and affording, at the same time, a solid hold to the hand.' Macnab added, 'All the weapons of this kind which are made here, or in the neighbouring mountains, are of the same form with these, and that from time immemorial.'

The sense of timelessness is thoroughly profound. But Highland society was changing rapidly and was overturning the ancient social order as conceived by the Celts. In the second half of the eighteenth century, a few lairds still kept smiths but they were no longer close members of the household and had lost their romantic status of 'armourer to the chief'. Professor Thomas Garnett (1766–1802), a Westmoreland chemist and physician, was another visitor to Glenorchy and found that although the Macnabs still made 'very beautiful highland dirks', their skills – even for 'meaner works' like the 'shoeing of horses' – were no longer in demand. The failure of the 'Forty-Five and the clearances had seen to that. Alexander Macnab (1747–1814), nephew of Malcolm, for a time succeeded in improving the fortunes of his family. Even so, after Malcolm's death in 1823 Barachastlain passed to another family and the Macnabs sought their fortunes abroad in North America, Australia and, ultimately, the Philippines. Everywhere the story was the same – history had moved briskly on, and the age of the clan *gobha* and the 'men of art' came to an end.

Kilchurn Castle, Loch Awe, stronghold of the Campbells of Glenorchy.

Chapter Four

FIREARMS AND THE LOWLAND AND BURGH WORKSHOPS

The mighty 'Mons Meg', cast at Mons by Jehan Cambier and a gift from the Duke of Burgundy to James II of Scotland in 1457. (Crown copyright: Royal Commission on the Ancient and Historical Monuments of Scotland)

I N 1537 John, Master of Forbes, was accused of having 'a design to shoot the King with a culverin as he passed through Aberdeen.' No evidence survives of a plot to kill James V (reigned 1513–42) with a 'culverin' – a type of long-barrelled hand-gun or cannon – but Forbes was put to death. This peculiar incident reminds us that even though Scotland's armies were often under-resourced, guns had become fairly abundant in the kingdom by the 1530s. Moreover, guns were now being made in Scotland, and James V presided over a modest but distinguished armaments industry based in the Lowlands. The main driver in injecting life into the industry was his father, James IV, a 'Renaissance prince' with wide interests spanning dentistry, ship-building, and architecture, as well as the military sciences.

THE 'MASTER MELTER'

Artillery, long a weak point in Scottish armies, was central to James IV's view of a new, powerful Scotland. Cannon had been used by the Scots since the 1380s, but no reference is made to gun-founding taking place in Scotland until 1473. This was during the reign of James III (reigned 1460–88), a supposedly unwarlike king who nevertheless spent £780 5s. 5d on artillery in the space of just over a year, some of this needed to repair the roof of a building probably used for cannon-making in the grounds of Blackfriars Priory, Edinburgh. Early gun-founding focused on Edinburgh but was sporadic, and it was another thirty or so years before production began on a sustained basis, first at Stirling *c.* 1507, and then once more at Edinburgh.

Robert Borthwick now emerges as a key figure, clearly a highly skilled engineer in the truest Scots tradition, who in 1511 was 'zettare of the Kingis gunnys' at James IV's new foundry in Edinburgh Castle. A year earlier, French gunners, including a certain Gerwez, had been sent to Scotland to work with Borthwick. They must have had to operate day and night to make all the cannon needed not only by the army, but also for James IV's other obsession, the navy. The *Michael*, launched at Newhaven in October of 1511, was, at around 1,000 tons, briefly the largest warship in northern Europe. Armed with twelve bronze cannon on each side and three giant 'basilisks' mounted on her bow and stern, she had a crew of 300 and a capacity to transport a further 1,000 or so soldiers. The *Michael* cost at least £30,000 to build and £500 a

Scots artillery of the sixteenth century in action. Sir James Hamilton of Finnart (centre) issues orders to a gun crew at the bridge of Linlithgow, scene of fighting in 1526 between James IV's widow, Margaret, and Archibald Douglas, Earl of Angus. A hand-gunner kneels by the fire to light a match-cord soaked in saltpetre needed to operate his arquebus. (Painting by Graham Turner)

Leather cannon, almost certainly made by James Wemyss (d. 1667), General of Artillery in Scotland and Master Gunner of England. Beneath a casing of leather, the barrel is made from a thin cylinder of sheet iron, beaten into shape and welded or patched along the joins, and reinforced with iron rings. Before leather casing was shrunk around the barrel, it was bound tightly with hemp cord. Though light enough to be moved by a single horse, leather guns lacked range and accuracy, and were liable to overheat. (West Highland Museum, Fort William)

month to run, at a time when annual royal income was £30,000–£40,000. During 1511–13 something like £8,710 was lavished each year on the navy – still, it was less than the £12,000 spent in 1502 on transporting and supplying 2,000 soldiers sent to help James's uncle King Hans of Denmark in an abortive campaign against the Norwegians and Swedes.

James IV's ships were crewed by expert foreign gunners: Hans, Jacob and Henrik 'Cutlug' from Flanders, and Guyane from France. Hans appears to have been the most senior among them, enjoying the rank of royal master gunner, a sort of inspector-general of artillery, and a role known since the reign of James IV's grandfather, James II, when William Bonar had occupied the position. The royal master gunner was separate from the master melter (head of gun-founding), and to the third great office of gun making, the master smith (head of gun tooling and finishing). Scots were beginning to build up a reputation as skilled gunners themselves. Hans had a Scotsman named Robert Herwort as his deputy, and in 1512 'Robert Borthwik, gunnar' was appointed 'maister meltare of the Kingis gunnis'. These specialists were clearly on good personal terms with James IV, and brief vignettes shine through the records of an excited James examining his wonder-weapons with his gunners: in 1504 Herwort rode with the King to inspect the fleet at Dumbarton; in 1506 Hans tested on Leith sands in the presence of James a gun made for the 600–700-ton *Margaret*, floated onto the Forth that year and named after James's wife.

The brass, bronze and iron that Borthwick was melting came largely from Flanders and France. The first cannon used in Scotland were made by tying iron rods round a wooden cylinder, which were then compressed with white-hot iron hoops. As the wooden core burnt away, the hoops and rods cooled, shrank and tightened into a sealed, hollow cannon barrel. James II was as fascinated by artillery as his grandson and imported iron cannon from the European continent. His most famous acquisition was the monster 'Mons Meg,' a gift in 1457 from Duke Philip 'the Good' of Burgundy.

Weighing in at over 6,000 kg and more than 4 metres long, Meg – the work of Jehan Cambier of Mons – remained the heaviest gun in the British Isles until the eighteenth century. Her ammunition was 150–200 kg stone balls shot to a range of 2.5 km. After eight or ten shots Meg had to be left to cool for the rest of the day. Meg was dragged out of Edinburgh Castle for the quashing of a rebellion in 1489 and for the siege of Norham Castle in 1497, and was last fired in 1681 to celebrate the birthday of James, Duke of York (later James VII and II), when her barrel ruptured. Iron cannon were prone to exploding, and Scotland's most famous fatality suffered this way was James II. When the Wars of the Roses broke out, James II had laid siege to Roxburgh Castle, for some time in English hands. Watching his beloved bombards go to work, one named the 'Lion' shattered, killing the king instantly.

Bronze has a greater malleability than iron, meaning there is less risk of metal fatigue, and less chance the gun will burst. Bronze cannon also had greater projectile power, leading James III to acquire some from abroad. By 1511 Scottish craftsmen were making their own, though the transition from iron to bronze had taken time, and de Ayala noted in 1498 that James IV still had 'old and heavy artillery of iron', though supplemented with 'modern French guns', presumably bronze, 'which are very good'. Iron instead became the material for cannon balls, superseding, during James IV's reign, balls of stone.

BOMBARDS AND CHURCH BELLS

During 1510–13, in the build-up to the Flodden campaign, extra cannon were bought over from France and Flanders, some from the Dutch founder Hans Popenruyter. The venerable Meg was probably considered too old and large to go with the Scots army to Flodden, but Borthwick commanded a battery that was almost as heavyweight: five 60-pound 'curtals', two 18- or 20-pound culverin, four 6- or 7-pound 'culverin pickmoyane', and six 4- or 5-pound 'culverin moyane'. Unfortunately, most of these guns were more suited to stationary siege-work, and

Iron barrel from a hand-cannon. Dug from the earth at Achnacarry, near the seat of Cameron of Lochiel. (West Highland Museum, Fort William).

Wemyss and his uncle Robert Scott (d. 1631), both Scotsmen, served in the Swedish army at a time when Gustavus Adolphus was experimenting with light artillery. Leather cannon were a Swiss invention and were introduced into Britain by Scott, and saw service during the Civil Wars. They were last used at Killiekrankie in 1689. (West Highland Museum, Fort William)

300–400 oxen, 29 pack horses, 26 gunners and as many as 300 drivers and pioneers were needed to transport or operate Borthwick's train.

Pointlessly huge and poorly deployed, Borthwick's guns at Flodden were a ludicrous failure. The smaller, more mobile guns of the 'Master Gonner of the Englishe', Hall recounts, 'bet all hys men from theyr ordinaunce, so that the Scottishe ordinaunce did no harme too the Englishemen'. But James was to blame, and his poor judgment at Flodden wasted what were magnificently crafted cannon (the 'finest that hath been seen', remarks Bishop Ruthal). By nightfall all Borthwick's guns were in English hands; Borthwick was lucky to escape with his life. He was not killed as Hall claims: post-Flodden, 'Robin of Borthwik' is noted in the treasurer's accounts as back at work constructing cannon in a new 'furnace in the castell of Edinburgh', receiving £100 as his 'yeris fee' until 1526. Around 1528 he was making church bells, including three signed by him for St Magnus, Kirkwall on Orkney. He was dead by 30 April 1532.

Scottish artillery put in a much better performance for the defence of Edinburgh in 1544, when an infant Mary, Queen of Scots was on the throne, and when Borthwick's old assistant Piers Rowane, 'Francheman' (d. *c.* 1548), was 'principale maister maker and maltar'. The Earl of Hertford led the English assault, managing to force his way into the city, getting dangerously near to Holyrood Palace. The big guns were brought down from Edinburgh Castle and positioned on the Royal Mile, from where they sent a hail of balls at the English. The Scots were pressed back and fighting spilt onto the High Street. Once again, Scotland seemed on the brink of collapse. But as Edinburgh's militiamen struggled with the English, the Scottish guns were pulled within the walls of Edinburgh Castle. Hamilton of Stonehouse got the artillery into position and supervised a steady fire, forcing the English to withdraw to Leith, laying waste to Edinburgh and the surrounding countryside as they went.

HAND-GUNS IN SCOTLAND

Records for the production of hand-guns in Scotland begin in the sixteenth century. They were in use in the country before then: Scottish soldiers are described as armed with them in 1489; during 1504–6 twenty-one small guns, probably 'hackbuts' (or possibly small-calibre swivel guns) were ordered for the *Margaret* at a cost of £20, and James IV obtained a hand-gun for himself in 1508. 'Hackbuts' or 'hagbushes' were the earliest type of hand-gun and were no more than small cannon on a stick, ignited by means of a smouldering match-cord. In 1510 James IV installed a Dutch or German craftsman named George Keppin and his servant Caspar Lepus at Edinburgh Castle to make hand-guns. James IV's royal cutler Robert Selkirk (d. 1512) worked on swords, armour, daggers and also guns. After James IV bit the dust at Flodden, Scottish gun making stagnated. Keppin and Lepus were still at work in Edinburgh in 1515, but the absence of royal patronage and direction – James V was only seventeen months old when his father died – seems to have meant Scottish gun-makers stuck to turning out obsolete hackbuts and culverins.

The situation improved as James V matured to manhood. He had his own hand-gun by 1533, for in that year he paid compensation to a man whose cow he shot; he acquired another from Rouen in 1537. Pistols and 'arquebuses' (forerunner of the musket) began to be made in Scotland from the middle of the sixteenth century. As early as 1549 two men, Francis Forcane and James Croiff, were prosecuted at Stirling for wounding a certain William Wycht, 'and schoting of his pistole'. An English spy report stated in 1575 that Edinburgh gunsmiths were capable of making fifty 'calivers' (light muskets) a week, adding that most Scottish gentlemen and horsemen already owned pistols or 'dags.' The earliest surviving Scottish-made guns, however, are a pair of pistols dated 1598, though four almost certainly Scottish gun barrels exist dated 1583, 1585, 1589 and 1595.

TOP
An iron-stocked scroll-butt pistol with snaphance lock, dated 1680, with maker's initials of 'I.S.' (possibly John Smith of Inverness). The ram rod is shown removed. (West Street Antiques, Dorking)

BOTTOM
Reverse of the pistol signed 'I.S.' The long metal hook running parallel to the barrel enabled the pistol to be suspended from a belt. (West Street Antiques, Dorking).

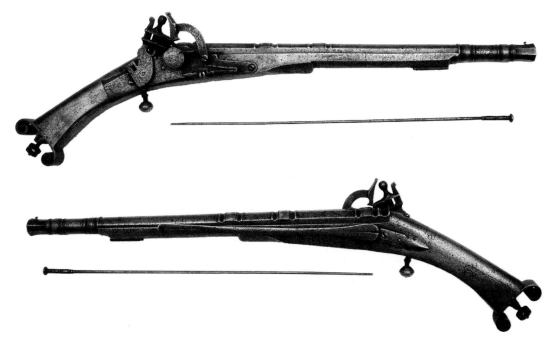

Scottish hand-guns become particularly distinctive during the seventeenth century with the production of all-metal pistols. These are characterised first by fish-tail or lemon-shaped butts. From about 1645–50 the fish-tail butt gives way to a more open, simpler scroll-shape, and heart-shaped butts take the place of the globular lemon-butt. The taste for pistols made entirely of metal – usually iron – arose partly from the gunsmiths' close links with the Incorporation of Hammermen, an old guild of smiths in existence since at least 1483. Restrictions imposed by the Hammermen may have meant gunsmiths were not allowed to make stocks from wood themselves, and so rather than give business to carpenters, they took on the job of stock-making themselves, albeit in metal. Wooden stocks had been made in Dundee and Edinburgh during the early days of gun making, and long-guns appear normally to have had stocks of wood, though not many survive. In Edinburgh and what was then the neighbouring burgh of Canongate, fruit wood was generally used for stocks, but in Dundee brazil wood was the norm, which was in easy supply since it was already imported by artisans to make red dye. As we have seen, hardwoods were scarce in Scotland – brazil wood is brittle – and the choice of metal stocks must also be seen in the context of gunsmiths searching for a stronger, more resilient alternative to the wood available in Scotland.

Wood-stocked snaphance long-gun of Sir Duncan Campbell, 7th Laird of Glenorchy (d. 1631). Dated 1599, it is the work of Patrick Ramsay of Dundee. (The Trustees of the National Museums of Scotland)

In the early seventeenth century, James Low of Dundee made guns entirely of brass, and even if the stock was wood, barrels of brass became common in Dundee, a town with a history of brass-working. Barrels of brass were made in Edinburgh and Canongate shortly after – around the 1620s – during which time the Edinburgh gun-makers gave up their association with the locksmiths to join with the lorimers who were known for their work in copper and brass. All-iron or brass guns, once made purely on the grounds of business and supply of materials, thereafter became both the fashion and the norm, and remained so until the Scottish gunsmithing workshops closed their doors for good in the late nineteenth century.

SIGNATURES AND MARKS

Before the 1680s, Scottish gunsmiths usually only marked their work with their initials. Later they began to sign with their full name, though unsigned guns continued to be made. Yet even when they did leave a name or initials, Scots gunsmiths all too often remain shadowy figures. Thus, James Low has been identified, with some good reason, as the maker of firearms marked 'I.L.', and 'D.H.' is probably David Howison of Auchinblae, Kincardineshire. Guns signed 'Pat MacNab' surely were made by one of the Patrick Macnabs of the Barachastlain family, and those signed 'MacNab' may be the work of Macnabs of Rannoch. Style can help, and some makers have what appears to be their own manner of working, but often we cannot be sure.

Other gunsmiths were at work in the Highlands besides Macnabs: the MacRurys of the isles and MacLeods of Suardal are said to have made guns for their respective clans; Hector MacNeil was a gunsmith on Mull in 1733, while William Smith of Duthel, Inverness-shire, received in 1675 a lease of land from the Chief of the Grants in return for his services as armourer and gunsmith. Two Highland towns, Inverness – capital of the Highlands – and Tain became important centres of gun making. All the same, most

Detail of portrait of Sir Evan MacGregor in 1822 (see p.106). Highland pistols were worn ostentatiously and hung, very often in pairs, by their loops on a waist belt. (Private collection)

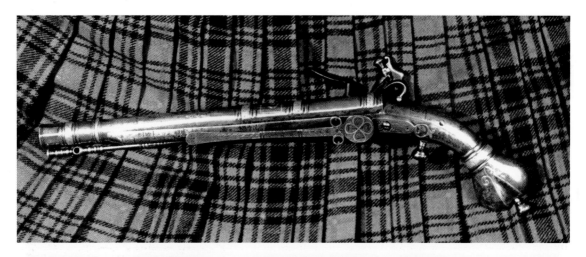

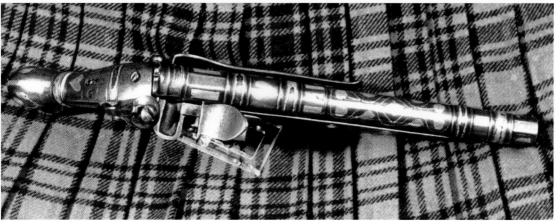

East Scots pistol of c. 1710 with heart-shaped butt, unsigned. The pistol's long belt loop is visible. (West Street Antiques, Dorking)

Scottish gun making took place in towns in the east and midland regions of Scotland, forming a ring of workshops around the Highlands. Their close proximity to the Highlands was not chance, as many of their clients were Highlanders, who eagerly sought guns for stalking and wild-fowling as well as feuding.

ORNAMENT AND DESIGN

Scottish pistols were usually made in pairs, one left-handed and the other right-handed, and hung on waist- and shoulder-belts from hooks fixed to the reverse side of the lock. Holsters were not used – a surprising decision given that Scottish guns were made without trigger guards, and that the trigger itself was only a little round button. But the danger of hanging such guns on belts was nullified by the guns being on display for all to see, an important consideration for the vain Highlander. Equally, Scottish pistols were small and straight enough to be stuffed into a plaid. Many men must have been injured or worse from their own pistols going off as they tore across the heather or scuffled in the alehouse.

The bullets Scottish pistols fired were of a very small calibre, and there are mixed reports as to their effectiveness as weapons. They certainly made fine costume accessories, and it was normal for engraved decoration to cover almost the whole pistol. This generally took the form of generic, pan-European engraved or gilded strap-work, foliage, scrolls, bands and floral ornaments. Thistles make an occasional appearance, as do engraved plaques bearing the owner's coat of arms. Every now and then stylised animals hark back to a Celtic manner of art still popular in the Highlands. Political views are expressed in tulips for William of Orange and Protestantism, the combination of a thistle and rose for loyalty to the Union, or the Virgin and saints for Catholicism. Sometimes the decoration has been carefully rendered; at other times it is pretty rough, but the overall impression would have pleased the average clansman who did not have much money to spend, but was keen to cut a military dash.

SNAPHANCE TO FLINTLOCK

By the late sixteenth century the wheel-lock was replacing the matchlock in Scotland, which in turn was replaced in about the 1640s by the 'snaphance' – a tremendous improvement on the unreliable matchlock and the complicated wheel-lock. Some early Scottish gunsmiths were men trained as locksmiths or blacksmiths. The links between locksmiths and gunsmiths is obvious, as the firing mechanisms of

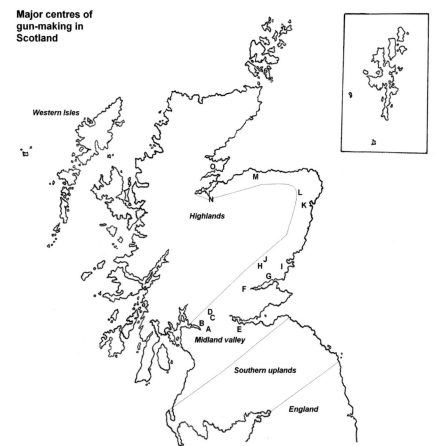

Major centres of gun-making in Scotland

Western Isles

Highlands

Midland valley

Southern uplands

England

Key to map:
A. Glasgow
B. Dumbarton
C. Doune
D. Stirling
E. Edinburgh
F. Perth
G. Dundee
H. Brechin
I. Montrose
J. Edzell
K. Aberdeen
L. Old Meldrum
M. Elgin
N. Inverness
O. Tain

Pistol, engraved and inlaid with silver, signed 'I. A. McKenzie' for James McKenzie of Brechin, c. 1700–10. (The Trustees of the Victoria and Albert Museum)

guns were complex and fiddly machines to make. The snaphance was a simple but ingenious mechanism in which a small piece of flint is clamped in the jaws of a sprung lever. When the trigger is pulled, the lever swings down onto a pan containing gunpowder. Sparks fly from the pan through a hole in the side of the barrel, igniting a charge of powder inside the barrel, thus forcing the bullet forwards. In the eighteenth century the snaphance was still made (quite late by European standards), even if the lock had become similar in appearance to the flintlock. The flintlock was effectively only a perfected, streamlined version of the snaphance, and at the close of the 1700s the snaphance was finally given up.

Guns, despite being relatively expensive, were much used by Highlanders. Doune in Perthshire became a main point of supply for the Highlands after the mid seventeenth century, in line with a general move of gunsmithing to the smaller towns. The industry at Doune, a mere village, probably began with Thomas Caddell who made iron scroll-butt pistols in the 1670s. He was followed by three generations of Caddells all named Thomas, while the families of Campbell and Murdoch (among others) then opened gun businesses in the town, and did well from a steady flow of Highlanders (and after the 'Forty-Five from sportsmen) coming to the town to buy or repair their guns. At the end of the eighteenth century, demand slackened off.

Sir John Sinclair's *Statistical Account of Scotland*, published in 1798, says gun making in Doune 'is now carried on by John Murdoch', a man 'famous for his ingenuity in the craft, and who likewise furnished pistols to the first nobility of Europe. These pistols were sold from 4–24 guineas a pair.' However, the *Statistical Account* adds:

> There is now very little demand for Doune pistols, owing, partly, to the low price of the pistols made in England, but the chief cause of the decline

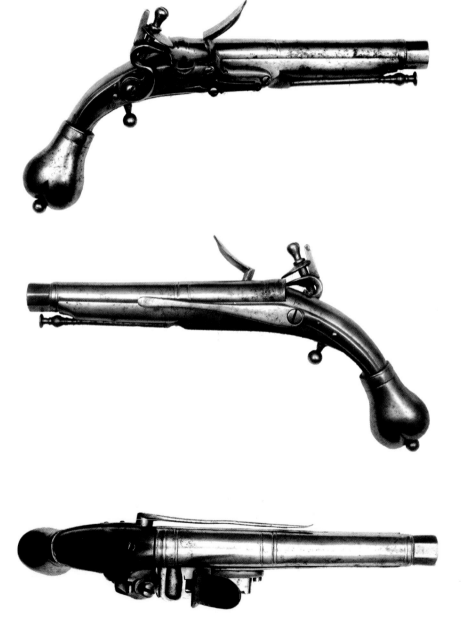

Four views of an east Scots pistol, c. 1720–30, perhaps by James McKenzie of Brechin. (West Street Antiques, Dorking)

Pistol, silvered decoration, by James Michie of Doune, c. 1750–80. (West Street Antiques, Dorking)

Pistol, one of a pair engraved and inlaid with silver, with signature 'I. O. Murdoch' of Doune, c. 1750–80. (The Trustees of the Victoria and Albert Museum)

Pistol, one of a pair engraved and inlaid with silver, with signature 'J. Patterson' of Doune, c. 1780–1800. (The Trustees of the Victoria and Albert Museum)

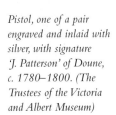

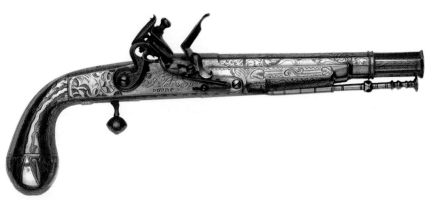

is the disuse of the dirk and pistol as a part of the Caledonian dress; and, when Mr Murdoch gives over the business, the trade, in all probability, will become extinct.

Dress and presentation pistols were still made and another John Murdoch actually kept the business afloat in Doune for many more years, though the pieces he made had become close to pure male jewellery.

HARNESS MILLS

In 1496 James IV established a 'harness mill', probably at Stirling. Little is known about the work carried out there, but there were already armourers active elsewhere in the Lowlands. The Moncurs of Dundee (a town receiving shipments of iron and hardwoods on a regular basis, as well as ready-made armour from the Low Countries and France) were an eminent family of armourers or military suppliers to the royal household. Legend says they were of French origin and that Michael de Moncur (b. *c.* 1165) met with David, Earl of Huntingdon (grandson of David I) in the Holy Land, leading to an invitation to work in Scotland as armourer to the King. What is known is that John Moncur of Dundee, *fabro armorum*, provided the Scottish court with armour from 1445, and some years later we hear of a William Moncur of Dundee, *factori armorum*. William died in 1471, when he is referred to by the Exchequer Rolls as *defuncto*, but another Moncur of Dundee was still working. In 1495, this latter 'Muncur of Dundee' supplied James IV with 'leg splentis and a pare of arme splentis', as he did again the following year.

As retained armourers to the king, the Moncurs, Selkirk and others probably imported, assembled and repaired as much armour as they actually made. A lack of familiarity among Scots with how to make plate armour is suggested by James IV's encouragement of French armourers to join his state workshops – one 'Laurence

Reverse of the pistol made by Patterson of Doune. (The Trustees of the Victoria and Albert Museum)

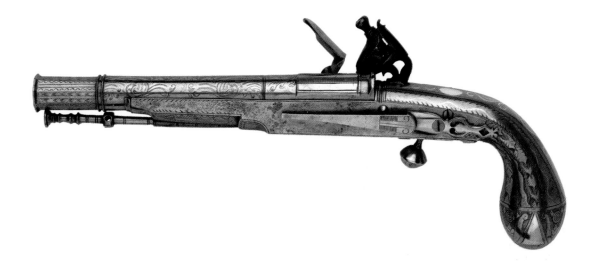

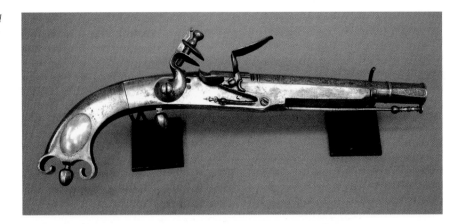

the Franch armorar' came over to Edinburgh in 1495 with Perkin Warbeck, tragicomic pretender to the English throne. Nevertheless, there was little obvious demand for full plate armour in Scotland. What plate armour was made was doubtless in time chopped up to make other equipment such as jacks, pieces of which do survive, and a type of armour generally more useful to the Scottish soldier than the heavy 'white harness'.

SWORD SLIPPERS

In Scotland most swordsmiths were actually 'sword slippers', from the German *Scheifer*, meaning an assembler and finisher of swords, who ground and sharpened sword blades and fitted them to hilts that he either made or bought from another supplier. There is no serious evidence that sword blades were ever made in Scotland, at least not in significant quantities, and nearly all came from Solingen (then part of Prussia) and other towns in Germany. A range of craftsmen produced elements of swords: Edinburgh had 'lorimers' who made all kinds of metal accessories such as

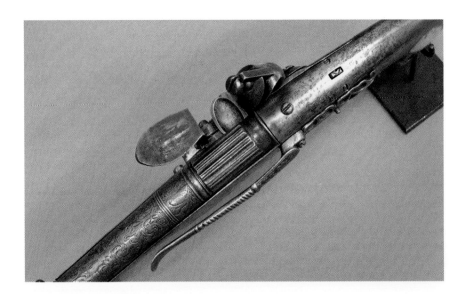

The pan and hammer of the same c. 1770 unsigned flintlock.

Flintlock mechanism of the c. 1770 unsigned pistol. (Michael German Antiques)

buckles, bits, spearheads and spurs and also hilts. Some cutlers, who usually produced knives, dirks and cutlery, also made swords, while 'buckle makers' supplied scabbards and dagger-sheaths from leather; some also made targes.

All slippers, lorimers and cutlers making swords belonged to the Hammermen, as membership was the only way a metalworker was allowed to practise his craft freely. The basket-hilted broadsword – an exceedingly deadly weapon we will later see in action – became a speciality of the urban Hammermen in the seventeenth century, with Stirling, Edinburgh and Glasgow being major centres of production. In the eighteenth century, John Allan the Elder, John Allan the Younger, Walter Allan and

Pistol engraved and inlaid with silver, signed T Mudoch' of Doune, late eighteenth century. (The Trustees of the Victoria and Albert Museum)

Scottish pistol of the 1820s or '30s, unsigned, probably made in Edinburgh. (Michael German Antiques)

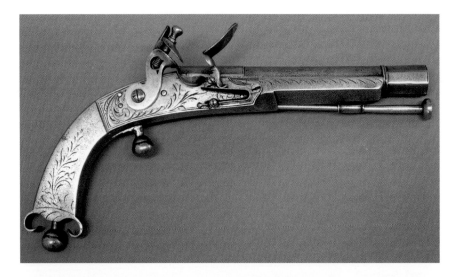

The unsigned 1820s–30s pistol viewed from above. (Michael German Antiques)

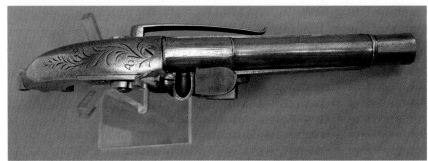

Reverse of the same 1820s–30s flintlock, showing its belt-loop. (Michael German Antiques)

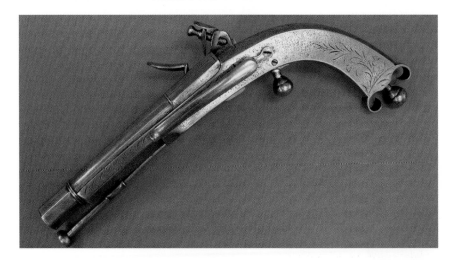

James Grant were the most famous sword slippers and hilt makers in Stirling, making 'claymores' from German blades set into strong iron hilts formed into a 'basket', imaginatively pierced and shaped with heart- and circle-shaped cut-outs.

John Simpson the Elder, John Simpson the Younger and Thomas Gemmill were equally renowned sword slippers and armourers in Glasgow. Gemmill had been admitted freeman in 1716 and two years later was made king's armourer. He was probably succeeded as armourer to the king by Simpson the Younger, already a freeman of Glasgow in 1711, and who died in 1749. His father, Simpson the Elder, was active from at least 1683 until about 1717, and his journeyman at one time may have been Allan the Elder. Upon qualifying as an armourer, Allan the Elder left Glasgow for Doune, where he seems to have been influenced by the decoration and ornament of the local gunsmiths, incorporating it into his own swords. In 1714, Allan the Elder, 'Sword slipper in Down' was admitted a burgess of Stirling; his son John was made burgess of Stirling in 1741.

The Hammermen of Glasgow made other weapons besides broadswords, including guns and targes. Guns and bows were made at Stirling too; polearms at Aberdeen, Leith and Jedburgh; almost anything could be ordered from the Lowland armourer, so long as the quantities required were low. This was as much a series of small-scale, home industries as the Highland smiths at work in their forges, the only difference being that there were simply more craftsmen in the Lowlands. General blacksmiths across the Lowlands were relied upon heavily to turn out polearms and other military basics. An interesting footnote to the failed Scottish Chartist rising of 1820 is the part played by Mackie's forge, a business founded in Aitken Street, Largs, in 1608 by Robert Mackie. A later Mackie is remembered as having made weapons at the forge for the rebels; the smithy was still going in the 1930s. The account of the blacksmith William Reid also survives. In 1715 Reid was employed by Dumfries town council for the 'shafting of 116 scythes', and to make pikes and halberds as the town prepared to face the Jacobites.

WEAPON-SMITHING IN THE JACOBITE AGE

By 1745 Lowland arms-making was already in decline. William Lindsey, a wright in Perth, produced 120 targes at around 5/- and £1 0s. 0d each for the Jacobites in 1745; so too did armourers and wrights in Edinburgh, but the rebel army remained chronically short of arms. Glasgow did not warm to the Jacobites as Edinburgh did. Yet whatever their political sympathies, most of the old guard of Lowland armourers went out of business after new, stronger, legislation was passed banning Highland dress and the ownership of arms in the Highlands. Walter Allan of Stirling (d. 1761), eldest son of John Allan senior, had supplied swords to the Jacobites but by 1748 was working for the military. Others found the transition harder, and armourers and craftsmen making edged-weapons proved on the whole less adaptable than gunsmiths. It was a sign of the times that by 1758 the Edinburgh armourer John Douglas was in prison for debt, representing a pitiful end to a Lowland industry that had flourished since the Middle Ages.

Chapter Five

UNION OF THE CROWNS

THE YEAR 1603 was a turning point in Scottish history. In that year King James VI of Scotland took the crowns of England and Ireland. His great-grandfather, James IV, had married Margaret Tudor, daughter of Henry VII of England, and when news reached James that Elizabeth I had died, he massed an army on the border and rode southwards. James did not need his army, and the various English claimants made way for the descendant of Kenneth MacAplin to take his place on their throne. Yet this was not to be an era of peace, but an age of chaos and civil war.

FLAT BLUE CAPS AND SAD-COLOURED CLOTHES

Lowlanders emerge in the early seventeenth century as extremely proficient and disciplined soldiers. The Lowlands were now largely Protestant, and religious sympathies moved thousands of young men to fight for the Dutch United Provinces against Catholic Spain, and for King Gustavus Adolphus of Sweden against the Holy Roman Empire. Come 1600 or so, jacks and basinets had fallen by the historical wayside to be supplanted by new modes of Lowland military costume. In 1598, an aristocratic Englishman named Fynes Moryson (1566–1630) rode from Berwick to Edinburgh and on to St Andrews, noticing that all the 'Husbandmen in Scotland, the servant, and almost all in the Country did weare course cloth made at home of gray or skie colour, and flat blew caps very broad.'

At the end of the seventeenth century this rather dour style of dress was still the norm. Thomas Morer, also an Englishman, was attached as chaplain to a Scots regiment in the war following William of Orange's 'glorious revolution' of 1688–91. He recalls that Lowlanders could be distinguished from Englishmen by the fact they wore 'bonnets instead of hats, and pladds instead of cloaks.' These 'bonnets or thrum-caps', Morer says, were 'not unlike those of our servitors, tho' of a better consistence to keep off the weather', being 'blue, grey, or sad-colour'd' and 'sometimes lined according to the quality of their master.' The sombre-coloured clothes Moryson and Morer saw were made from an inexpensive undyed cloth known as 'hodden grey', a term referring to a range of shades from dark charcoal through to brownish-grey. It had begun as the cloth of the simple countrymen but, with the large blue bonnet of knitted wool, became the distinguishing colour of seventeenth-century Lowland armies.

THE INFLUENCE OF SWEDEN

In 1639 a rebellion broke out in Scotland following an attempt by Charles I to force Presbyterians to adopt a new prayer book based on the model used in England.

OPPOSITE
Late seventeenth-century targe from the armoury of the Lairds of Grant; made from two layers of wood, reinforced with an iron plate, tooled leather, brass studs and a boss. (The Trustees of the National Museum of Scotland).

King James VI of Scotland from 1567, and I of England and Ireland, 1603–25. (John Wesley's House and the Museum of Methodism)

Alexander Leslie, Earl of Leven (*c.* 1580–1661), who had served with distinction in the Dutch army and under Gustavus, was appointed military commander of the 'Covenanters', as those who pledged to defend the Presbyterian faith were known. The heart of Covenanting country was the southwest, a region of stolid gentleman-farmers, lairds and freeholders with a long tradition of dissent – but most lacked military experience. Leslie ambitiously organised his army along modern Swedish lines, relying on drill, musketry and pike, usually at a ratio of about two musketeers to every one pikeman.

Leslie's men were issued with hodden grey uniforms issued from government central stocks. The choice of grey was one of money (it was the cheapest cloth available), not ideology. Not all Scottish regiments wore grey, and the 'Minister's Regiment' of the Civil War years was so-named because its uniforms were made, it is said, from second-hand clerical clothing. Some Royalists may have worn the Stuart colours of red and yellow. When Charles II was restored to the throne in 1660, a greater range of colours was introduced. In the ballad of Bothwell Bridge (1679) we hear of Scots militia with 'coates of blew', but even at that time hodden grey remained the defining colour of the Scottish army. 'Hodding gray' is among the plunder taken by Highlanders from southwest Scots listed by Lieutenant Colonel Cleland in his mock poem recounting anti-Covenanter policing by Highland soldiers in 1678. It was only in 1684 that the Privy Council permitted merchants to import red cloth from England. Hodden grey had evidently retained the stigma of being the yokel's cloth, since the same year the Privy Council requested cloth-merchants and weavers to supply 'sufficient cloathes at reasonable rates and of such dye as shall be thought fit to distinguish sojers from other skulking and vagrant persons'.

Covenanter's banner, said to have been carried at the battle of Drumclog in 1679, a victory for the soldiers of the Covenant. (East Ayrshire Arts and Museums)

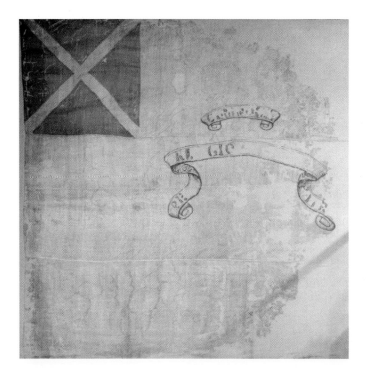

PIKE AND MUSKET

The pikeman was an essential component in this new type of army. Armed with a 16–18-foot pike and a sword, his job was to defend the musketeers as they loaded and fired. The armour of the Covenanter or Scots Parliamentarian pikeman was, in theory, a breast- and sometimes back-plate, with perhaps a buff-coat of leather or 'gorget' for the throat. Some, especially officers, had 'pot' helmets, but rarely was the complete 'corselet' seen in Scotland. Old helmets must have been used, but new German helmets of *Zischägge* form and 'Dutch pots' were also imported. In contrast, musketeers rarely wore armour. Their weapon was the heavy matchlock. The musket of the period had a range of about 100 metres and a rate of fire of little more than one round a minute, but it was a devastating weapon when used in massed volleys – this was a weapon that could leave an exit wound the size of a dinner plate. One Scots regiment at Dunbar was armed with 'firelocks', but usually these were issued only to infantry detailed to guard artillery, where the presence of burning match-cords needed for the matchlock would be dangerous.

The officers brought their own swords with them, while many were also armed – as were sergeants – with halberds and partisans. Perhaps a few still had 'dudgeon daggers' too. Dudgeon daggers were made by craftsman in Canongate during the first two or three decades of the seventeenth century, and bear a close resemblance to their medieval forebear, the 'ballock' knife. Their hilts were cylindrical or octagonal and carved from solid native boxwood, into which was set a thick chisel-like blade,

The Scots lines at Dunbar, 1650. (Painting by Graham Turner)

An ensign, drummer and pikeman of the Strathbogie regiment, 1644. Raised in 1639 as a Royalist unit, the Strathbogie regiment occupied Aberdeen in 1644 and fought with distinction at Auldearn in 1645. Here, their standard-bearer carries Scotland's royal standard with added slogans to indicate their loyalty to their country's royal family. (Painting by Graham Turner)

almost always double-edged and diamond-shaped in cross section, and etched with decoration and mottoes.

Leslie's reforms were far-reaching. He built up a respectable artillery train, manned with regulars rather than mercenaries and contracted civilians. On the whole, these were sound decisions. If, however, the men were shaky, ill-trained or fighting against an opponent who did not play by the modern Swedish and Dutch rules – like the Highlanders, who still preferred massed infantry charges and man-on-man duels – there was a severe risk that their lines would collapse. At Tippermuir (1644) novice soldiers fled in panic from Royalist Highlanders led by the (Presbyterian) Marquis of Montrose, James Graham (1612–50). Montrose's army was less than half the size of the Covenanter army, and some of his Highlanders were armed only with stones.

Raw animal aggression could still defeat modern technology and the Highlanders tore apart the Covenanters, killing a dozen in the battle and 2,000 in the pursuit.

Even so, the advantages of Leslie's reforms became in the long run obvious, as drill, logistics, supplies and recruitment were all, for the first time, made real priorities. Even if many of Leslie's men lacked training, and even though some were poorly armed, there was an inner strength to their organisation that previous Scottish armies had lacked. At times, too, the Covenanters, who wore a blue ribbon to mark their adherence to the cause, showed themselves to be fanatical fighters quite ready to die to defend the Calvinist Reformation in Scotland. The first Covenanter rising ended inconclusively in June 1640, but by August, Leslie was marching on Newcastle at the head of 20,000 Covenanters. Civil war engulfed England and Ireland, and Leslie became commander of Scottish forces in an alliance with the English Parliamentarians.

ABOVE
Two-handed sword of 'clam-shellit' type, c. 1600–20; German blade on Scottish hilt. (The Master and Liverymen of the Worshipful Company of Armourers and Brasiers)

ABOVE AND RIGHT
'Clam-shellit' two-handed sword (grips missing), c. 1600–20. In the seventeenth century plate armour began to disappear from the battlefield. Soldiers were less likely to wear gauntlets, leading to the development of sword guards offering a higher degree of protection to the hands, like basket-hilts and these twin-cup 'shells'. (East Ayrshire Arts and Museums)

CAVALRY

An unusual sight in Scottish armies during the Civil War, or 'War of the Three Kingdoms,' was the lancer. The lancer had vanished from English armies, but units of Scottish lancers fought all through the Civil War era, and they showed themselves to be quick, manoeuvrable and with some impressive shock capability. At Preston (1648) it was Royalist Scots lancers, equipped very much in the vein of the old Border reivers, who threw back Parliament's advance with a spirited counter-attack. Scots lancers achieved the same at Dunbar two years later. Regiments of dragoons – horsemen armed with swords, axes, war-hammers, wheel-lock pistols and carbines – were raised by Leslie (himself an old cavalryman) in 1643, most of whom wore the same grey, with breast, back and 'pot'. The Royal Scots Dragoons, the most famous of Scottish dragoon regiments, were raised in 1678, at which time they dressed in grey. This may be the origin of their title 'Scots Greys', and not, as later, because they rode grey horses. The ever-dashing Ogilvys and Gordons, whose intervention was critical in breaking up the Covenanters at Auldearn (1645), provided a few cavalry for the Royalist war effort in the Highlands.

Helmet, said by tradition to have belonged to Montrose; German or Dutch, c.1640s. (West Highland Museum, Fort William)

HIGHLAND BATTLE-DRESS

Charles I still had supporters in Scotland and these tended to be found in the Highlands, where Montrose and Alisdair MacColla (d. 1647) operated with magnificent panache. Their army, never much exceeding 4,000 men, was made up of Irishmen and anti-Campbell Highlanders – MacDonalds, Gordons, MacGregors, MacLeans, Ogilvys and others. Their appearance was strikingly different from Leslie's army, and was described by the Covenanter general William Baillie as 'but a pack of naked runagates, not three horse among them, few either swords or musquetts.' Highlanders fought on both sides in the Civil War: Campbells, MacKenzies and MacLennans died in substantial numbers for the Covenant at Auldearn. Earlier in the year Montrose and MacColla's soldiers had been only too pleased to manure the field of Inverlochy not with 'sheep dung', as Iain Lom (*c.* 1624–*c.* 1710), bard of Keppoch, put it, but with 'Campbell blood after congealing.' The Campbell chief, the Marquis of Argyll, commanded the Covenanting army at Inverlochy, skulking aboard a galley moored on the nearby loch as his clansmen were hewn apart in a flurry of claymore blows.

Montrose and MacColla were fortunate to have Irishmen, who, equipped in much the same way as the Covenanters with pikes and muskets, were part of a transformation of the native Irish from kern to well-trained infantrymen, taking the example presented by their English adversaries as inspiration. No such change had taken place in the Highlands, where watching stags rut and wild-cats stalk the heather were more influential lessons in military science than manuals on the latest approaches to drill and tactics. As natural warriors rather than regular soldiers, the Highlanders still went to war in their ordinary clothes; the only 'uniforms' Montrose and MacColla were able to grant their men were stalks of oats plucked from the fields. Daniel Defoe (*c.* 1660–1731) writes in his *Memoirs of a Cavalier*, apparently with some authority, of 'the oddness and barbarity of their garb' as they progressed through England in 1639. Though 'uncouth' (a word Defoe uses to describe the Lowlanders too), Highland costume 'seemed to have something in it remarkable.' Defoe adds, 'They were generally tall swinging fellows' that 'looked when drawn out like a regiment of Merry-Andrews ready for Bartholomew fair.'

But the sight of Highlanders on the attack was anything but comical. The *Hind Let Loose*, a poem written at the time of the Covenanter rebellions, calls the Highlanders 'more terrible than Turks or Tartars'. We have already heard twice from Cleland's poem about Highlanders stationed in south-west Scotland during 1678, lest, the government feared, 'the phanaticks in the west should rise in armes'. They did, and would carry on the fight into the 1680s. The verse of Cleland, an officer in Lord Angus' regiment, is crowing, though the vital point is made that it was the Highlanders 'who led the Van, and drove the Rear' of the king's army. This had been the role of Highlanders and galloglass since medieval times. Agile yet heavily armed, it was still a responsibility best entrusted to Highlanders. Of Highland dress the same poem says:

With good blew Bonnets on their Heads:
Which on the one side had a flipe,
Adorned with a Tobacco pipe,
With Durk, and Snap work, and Snuff-mill,
A bagg which they with Onions fills,
And as their strick observers say,
A Tupe Horn filled with Usquebay [whisky]
A slasht out Coat beneath her plaides,
A Targe of timber, nails and hides
With a long two handed Sword,
As good's the Country can afford...

HIGHLAND TARGES AND ARMOUR

Put simply, the Highlanders were the best-equipped soldiers in seventeenth-century Britain. Added to which, they were the only people who still made military training an essential part of a man's upbringing. However, if contemporary descriptions provide a consistent portrait of Highland clothes and arms, we are presented with a more confused picture when it comes to the use of armour. Most accounts of the

Dirk, bog-oak hilt, and steel blade made from a cut-down blade from a two-handed or broad-edged sword, c. 1660–80. (East Ayrshire Arts and Museums)

A Highland gentleman, identified as Sir Mungo Murray (1668–1700), by John Michael Wright (1617–94). (Scottish National Portrait Gallery)

time do not mention armour; by now galloglass had disappeared from the scene too, and in 1618 Thomas Gainsford, veteran of Kinsale (1601), gave these impressive axe-men the puny epitaph that 'the name of galloglas is in a manner extinct'.

Yet, quite old-fashioned armour of the 'three heroes' variety used by galloglass was clearly regarded as worth keeping, and on occasions apparently still used – though probably not to the degree claimed by an account of the Highlanders in the south-west in 1678 in which the Highland men wear 'strange pieces of armour mentioned in our old lawes, such as bosnet, iron-hat, gorget, pesane, warmbrassers an reerbrassers, panns, leg-splents, and the like'. A survey conducted in 1638 of 'vapins and armour' in four Perthshire parishes found that 523 men had between them eleven mail shirts, one jack, eight 'head pieces', two 'steel bonnets' and a set of 'pleat sleives'. Whether or not the men of Perthshire planned to use these items in the coming war we cannot say, but it is not inconceivable that Highlanders should now and then dig out the old basinets and mail, perhaps to frighten local civilians or to guard against Covenanter snipers. We do know that at Killiekrankie in 1689 Viscount Dundee wore an iron cuirass and helmet (they did not save him from death), just as leather jerkins were still used in the early eighteenth century.

It was the targe that now more commonly satisfied the need for bodily defence. The targe was small but Morer claims Highlanders had 'such artificial way of twisting themselves within the compass of these shields' that their opponents seek in vain 'to annoy 'em.' Morer goes on to say that the Highland targe was 'so serviceable that no ordinary bullet, much less a sword, can penetrate to injure them'. The targe's strength and durability was derived from its many layers. A letter dated 1716 from Henry Fletcher to his brother, Andrew Fletcher of Saltoun, gives an important description of the construction of the targe, saying by way of introduction that 'ane Highland Targe is a convex circle, about 2 foot in diameter, but some have them oval'. The foundations of the targe were two layers of wood (Fletcher says birch was used, but other varieties were too), stuffed full of wool. On the side of the targe facing the man's breast a steel plate was fixed, to which two handles were attached. The whole structure was then covered with leather (this could be deer, pig or cow-hide), with the hair left upon the part of the skin used

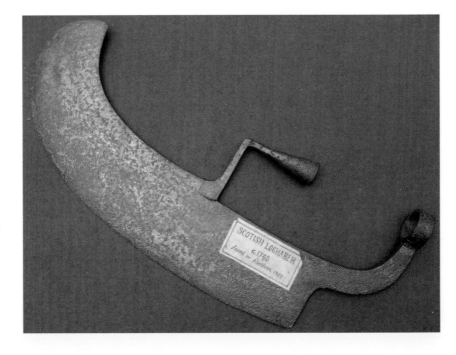

Lochaber axe-head, c.1660–1700, with label saying it was found in 1907 in 'Aberdean'. Aberdeen appears to have been a centre for the production of Lochaber axes: in 1715 the Jacobite Earl of Mar ordered 'the magistrats of Aberdeen to cause make three hundred Lochaber axes', which were then to be sent to his encamped army. (West Street Antiques, Dorking)

for the side of the targe bearing the carrying handles. The other side of the targe was, Fletcher continues, 'covered with plain well-wrought leather, which is nailed to the Cork with nails' with 'very hard brass heads'. These nails could 'sometimes throw off a ball, especially when it hits the Targe a squint'. From the centre of the targe 'sticks out a Stiletto … which fixes into the Steel plate and wounds the Enemy when they are close.' Fletcher goes on:

> … about this Stiletto closs to the Targe ther is a peece of Brass in the form of a cupelo about 3 inches over and coming half way out on the Stiletto … Within this brass ther is a peece of Horn of the same forme like a cup, out of which they drink their usquebaugh, but it being pierced in the under part by the Stiletto, when they take it off to use it as a cup they are obliged to apply the forepart of the end of their finger to the hole to stop it, so that they might drink out of their cup.

WHISKY AND TARTAN

Whisky toasting was (and still is) an important ritual in Scotland. Every visit to another's house and any public occasion called for a glass raised. That is not to say that the Highland charge was carried out by men who were drunk – but a dram before combat must have gone a long way to instil the right kind of mood needed for the launching of a wild head-on attack. A more refined development was the adoption of hats by Highlanders. In the sixteenth century Highlanders are generally described as bare-headed, but in the early years of the next century they evidently took a fancy to the Lowlandman's bonnet and began wearing, quoting again from Defoe, 'a cap on their heads, called by them a bonnet'. A representative summary of Highland dress in its complete form is given by the eccentric John Taylor (*c.* 1578–1653), a Thames waterman and poet, in his account of a journey to Scotland:

> Their habite is schooes with but one sole apiece; stockings (which they call short hose) made of a warm stuffe of diverse colours, which they call Tartane: as for breeches, many of them, nor their forefathers, never wore any, but a jerkin of the same stuffe that their hose is of, their garters being bands or wreathes of hay or straw, with a plead about their shoulders, which is a mantle of diverse colours, much finer and lighter than their hose, with blue flat caps on their heads, a hankerchief knit with two knots about their necke; and thus they are attyred … As for their attire any man of what degree soever that comes amongst them, must not distaine to weare it.

Magnificent in the great kilt, the *fèileadh-mòr* and *plaid* ('blanket'), or in tight *truibhs* ('trews'), and customarily a short jacket cut from *breacan* (tartan, from the word for 'speckled'), in the early years of the 1600s the Highlanders blossomed into the tartan-clad heroes that are today so celebrated. It is important to note here that clan tartans did not exist. That said, we can detect the beginnings of clan and district colours. James Philip of Almerieclose refers to clansmen gathered at Dalcomera in 1689 wearing plaids marked with thin stripes of a colour demonstrating allegiance to a particular chief. Militiamen of Clan Grant were ordered in 1704 to have 'Heighland coates, trewes, and shorthose of tartan of red and greine sett broad-springed'. About a decade earlier Martin wrote that Gaels were able 'at the first view of a Man's Plad, to guess the Place of his Residence'. Royal interest in tartan did not begin with Victoria: James V went hunting in tartan in 1538 and Charles II wore tartan ribbons on his coat at his wedding in 1662.

BROADSWORDS

Swathed in tartan, the Highlander would festoon himself with as many weapons as he could possibly carry. Highland swords were no longer like those of their medieval forebears. In the mid sixteenth century, basket-hilted swords had begun to be used in Scotland. Its roots lay in continental Europe, but from the seventeenth century it became a decidedly Highland weapon, with a huge blade of positively 'halflang' dimensions, either 'broad' (double-edged) or 'backed' (sharp on one side only) – often 'extravagantly and I think insignificantly broad' in Defoe's opinion. This was the true claymore, and the word itself was a Highland battle-cry.

The two-handed sword was still used, and would be until the late seventeenth century. Around 1600 the older Highland and Lowland varieties had been joined by a new type of two-handed sword. This was the 'clam-shellit' two-hander, so-named because of the clamshell-like guard that had been added to give extra protection to the hand. Yet again, their blades are usually German. Two-handed swords were used less and less as the century wore on. In the Perthshire survey of 1638 only three diehards are listed as having a 'tua handit swird' (the word claymore is not used) among 523 men, though this had probably always been about the ratio of two-handed swords to single-handed swords in Highland retinues. If we add in the eleven pole-axes and halberds (probably Lochabers in many cases) also included in the roll, we can see a continued preference for making a hard assault with a vanguard armed with two-handed weapons.

The same survey also counts 448 men owning swords, and even if some of these were perhaps dirks, when we include the 125 who also had a 'tairge', a picture of a new type of Highland warrior emerges: a man armed with a broadsword and targe – an excellent combination of arms for a people who relied so heavily on the charge. These two tools of war now became the mark of the gentleman. For the ordinary Highlander, as revealed in the above survey, 'bowis' and 'sheavis' (149 of them) were still more common than guns (110 'gunes with snap warkis'). Taylor also found some Highlanders to be armed (for hunting!) with swords and 'targets', but notes others

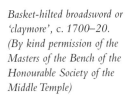

Basket-hilted broadsword or 'claymore', c. 1700–20. (By kind permission of the Masters of the Bench of the Honourable Society of the Middle Temple)

to be armed with bows, 'durks' and 'Loquhabor-axes'. It is these latter items we should consider typical weaponry for the common clansman.

The hand that held the targe also often gripped a dirk, with blade pointed downwards. Richard James (1592–1638), another English traveller, visited Scotland around 1617, noting that Highlanders carried a 'long kind of dagger broad in the back and sharp at ye point which they call a durcke.' Morer remembers that Highlanders were seldom seen, 'though only taking the air, without sword and dirk'. Despite its bucolic origins, the dirk emerged as a thing of considerable craftsmanship during the seventeenth century. With a long, flat blade, the dirk formed an important part of the Highland fighting technique, and was probably used to parry blows, and to hook away enemy blades. Effectively a short sword, it was also kept ready in one hand in case the broadsword should fall from the warrior's hand or be broken. In addition, a well-armed Highlander would carry a brace of pistols. Highlanders often had better guns – nearly always snaphances – than those issued to the average soldier of the day, even if a degree of retention of obsolete firearms is hinted at by Taylor's reference to not only muskets but also arquebuses, while the Perthshire survey lists two 'hagbutts'. Firearms were not considered manly enough to warrant much attention from the bards (unlike the bards' favourite instrument of death, the sword). The warrior and bard Do'ull MacIain 'ic Sheumais, victor of the battle of Carinish (1601), nevertheless does make a reference to guns in a song to his grandson:

> Son of blue eyes of Moidart,
> It was not the dark fumes of the mill-dust
> That you were accustomed to in your father's house,
> But young men burning gun-powder [*losgadh fùdair*],
> With mirth, joy and festivity.

THE FIRST JACOBITE RISING

The formidable energy and edged weaponry of the Highlanders opened the first Jacobite rising with a stunning victory at Killiekrankie in 1689. This was civil war, not war with England, though relations with the 'auld enemy' were hardly amicable. Scots Parliamentarians had been outraged that they were not consulted over the decision to behead Charles I in 1649; the next year Leslie and Oliver Cromwell, former allies, fought each other at Dunbar, Cromwell declaring to Parliament that God made the Scots 'as stubble to our swords.' Neither was the union of the crowns proving beneficial to Scotland. Consequently, when James VII of Scotland and II of England (reigned 1685–8) was deposed by his son-in-law William of Orange (reigned 1689–1702), many Scotsmen – Presbyterians, Episcopalians and Catholics alike – turned out in force.

At Killiekrankie, John Graham, Viscount Dundee (1648–89) led 2,500 Jacobites, as supporters of King James (*Jacobus* in Latin) were known, against 4,000 Williamites under a Sutherland man, Hugh Mackay of Scourie (*c.* 1640–92). Most of Dundee's men were Highlanders with some Irishmen and Lowlanders. Mackay was a Highlander himself and describes the standard tactic of his people in his memoirs: after firing once or twice, Highlanders 'throw away their firelocks, and everyone drawing a long broad sword, with his targe … they fall a running toward the enemy.' But Mackay had spent too much time serving on the European continent and had forgotten how battles were won in the Highlands. The plug-bayonets used by his men were no match for claymores. Sir Ewen Cameron of Lochiel (1629–1719) led his clan barefooted at the battle, and recalls that his men 'fell in pell-mell among the thickest of them with their broadswords'. A strange quiet, Lochiel remembers, descended across the battlefield, 'the fire ceasing on both sides', and 'nothing was heard' save for 'the sullen and hollow clashes of broadswords, with the dismall groans and crys of dyeing and wounded men.'

Dundee was mortally wounded in the attack, but within minutes his Jacobite warriors had won the battle. Lochiel recounts the horror of their victory, seeing on the field of battle 'the dreadful effects' of the Jacobites' 'fury'. The enemy 'lay in heaps allmost in the order they were posted', some with 'their heads divided into two halves by one blow', and others with 'their sculls cutt off above the eares by a back-strock'. The corpses of Mackay's men were, Lochiel continues, 'so disfigured with wounds, and so hashed and mangled' that not even the Highlanders could look at what they had done, at the 'amazeing proofs' of their 'agility and strength', without 'surprise and horrour.'

The Jacobites reported to James that they had killed three-quarters of the Williamites 'under the weight of our swords' – it was true: nearly all of them were killed with hand-weapons. The tools to commit such slaughter were the same as those of Montrose and MacColla's time: broadswords, dirks, targes and Lochaber axes. The battle, on the other hand, was the beginning of the most famous period of Scottish arms and armour: the Jacobite Wars.

An allegory of Union from William Guthrie's General History of Scotland *(1767), depicting Britannia 'in the action of reconcilling' a 'Scotch Warrior' and an 'English Baron'. (John Wesley's House and the Museum of Methodism)*

Chapter Six

THE JACOBITE WARS

ADISPLAY CASE in the National Museum of Scotland houses the sword and targe of Prince Charles Edward Stuart (1720–88), grandson of James VII and II. These are the relics of a man who on 20 September 1745 declared to an army of Jacobite clansmen, 'Gentlemen, I have flung away the scabbard; with God's help I will make you a free and happy people.' When these words were translated into Gaelic, the Highlanders gave an almighty cheer and tossed their bonnets into the air. The next day the Jacobites, most of whom were Highlanders, won a swinging victory at Prestonpans, defeating a larger army of government soldiers in a matter of minutes. The tactical instinct of the Highlanders remained as ever to rock the enemy with furious charges, and if that failed, to melt into the hills and harass the enemy until he withdrew. Reverend Alexander Carlyle (1722–1805), Minister of Inveresk, was a Hanoverian volunteer during the 1745–6 rising and summarises what happened at Prestonpans: 'After firing once, they Run on with their Broadswords, and our People Fled.'

THE DECLINE OF WARRIOR SOCIETY

The Stuart risings are the endpoint of most of what we have been tracing over the course of this book. We have now reached the final, epic act in the history of traditional Scottish arms and armour, since this was the last occasion that the Highland clans would raise their feudal levies, and take to the battlefield not in uniforms, but in tartan plaids and bonnets, wielding claymores, targes and dirks. The aim of the Jacobites was to restore the Stuarts to the British throne, and unsuccessful attempts were made to restore James VII and II and later his son, also named James, in 1689, 1708, 1715 and 1719. The most determined of these attempts was made in 1745, with the intention of unseating George II, son of the 'wee German lairdie', George of Hanover. This last rising was led by Prince Charles and his two lieutenant-generals, Lord George Murray (1694–1760) and James Drummond, Duke of Perth (1713–46).

The Stuarts' best chance of success lay with the Highlanders, and the Highland clan regiments would form in every rising the van of the Jacobite army. But modernity had begun to touch the Highlands. By 1745, it was now no longer the case that every clansman was a well-armed warrior. Disarming Acts passed in 1716 and 1725 made it illegal to bear arms in the Highlands. Both pieces of legislation were largely ignored and weapons were hidden away, but more damaging was a general sense that the clans and kin-society were beginning to break down. The mutual loyalty binding chief with clansman was weakening, and some chiefs, succumbing to materialistic ambitions, were coming to regard their clansfolk as a burden rather than a source of pride. Furthermore, open warfare between clans had petered out as central government and law and order penetrated the Highlands. The Highlands were no longer the private tribal redoubt they had once been, and clanship could not survive for long under these conditions.

OPPOSITE
A typical basket-hilted broadsword of the later Jacobite period. Its hilt would have been made in a Lowland town, and fitted to a blade probably made in Germany (though it bears the spurious signature of Andrea Ferrara). The guard is lined with leather and fabric padding.

Backsword and targe of
Prince Charles Edward
Stuart, used at Culloden.
The targe is made from
overlapping wooden
boards covered in pigskin,
to which have been added
classically inspired silver
mounts – battle-standards,
drums, trumpets, swords,
palm leaves, quivers of
arrows – centring on the
head of Medusa. The
mounts were probably the
work of a London smith.
In 1740 the targe and
sword were given to
Charles by James,
3rd Duke of Perth. The
sword has a silver basket-
hilt made by the London
smith Charles Frederick
Kandler. The sword was
lost at Culloden and
presented as a gift to the
Duke of Cumberland.
The targe was rescued
from the battlefield by the
Jacobite colonel Ewan
MacPherson of Cluny
(d. 1764). It remained in
Cluny's family until the
twentieth century. (The
Trustees of the National
Museum of Scotland)

Scottish powder horn of
flattened cow horn. Many
were made at home by
Highlanders, but
professional horn-makers
existed: among the rebels
of the 1745–6 rising was
Marmaduke MacBeath,
'Powder Flask Maker, of
Canongate'. (West Street
Antiques, Dorking).

The simple chiselled
decoration, and initials of the
owner 'W. I.', and date of
manufacture '1726', are
common features of Scots
powder horns of the period.
(West Street Antiques,
Dorking)

Targe, bearing date '1708' and owner's initials 'W. M.' The central boss is missing. (The Trustees of the Victoria and Albert Museum)

The reverse of the 'W. M.' targe. The back layer of leather and arm-loops are missing, revealing its inner construction — an outer layer of very thick leather covers a lining of coarse fabric, nailed over wood. (The Trustees of the Victoria and Albert Museum)

CLAN ARMIES

On the whole, it was the smaller, Catholic, Episcopalian or otherwise marginalised clans that came out for the Stuarts (Camerons, Chisholms, Farquharsons, Fletchers, MacDonalds, MacGregors, MacKinnons, MacLeans, MacPhersons, Ogilvys, Stewarts of Appin, among the other usual suspects), while the larger clans either stayed at home or were actively pro-government (Campbells, Mackays, Munros, Rosses, Sutherlands). Others (MacLeods, Macnabs and Mackintoshes) were divided. The Lowlands were even more divided. Among Jacobites in both the Lowlands and Highlands, nostalgic loyalty for the old Stuarts intermingled with resentment towards the Act of Union of 1707, which had transformed Scotland and England from two countries ruled by one king into a single nation with a single parliament in Westminster. In some respects, the Jacobite army of the 'Forty-Five rising was the

Charles Edward Stuart,
by Robert Ronald McIan
(1803–56).

last Scottish army. Many, if not most, Scots were loyal Hanoverians, and many Englishmen (particularly in the northwest) joined with the Jacobites, but the Highland clans were the mainstay, the beating heart, of the Jacobite cause. These clans were not fighting to reinstate a Stuart king based in London, but to bring a Stuart king back to Holyrood Palace, to rule over an independent Scotland.

ARMS OF THE HIGHLAND ARISTOCRACY

The problem was that by 1745 only the chiefs, tacksmen and the warriors in their immediate circle could be counted upon to be well armed. It was still taken for granted in the Highlands that a chief would be commander of his clan 'regiment', and that his officers would be members of his family or his most trusted tacksmen. For its part, the Highland officer class was splendidly turned out for the Jacobite risings. Carlyle writes of one Jacobite gentleman he encountered, 'a Fine Brisk little well Dress'd Highlander', who was 'arm'd Cap a Pie with Pistols and Dirk and Broadsword.' Carlyle explains the man's position in Charles' army: 'He said he had that Morning been Armour Bearer to the Duke of Perth, whose Valour was as Conspicuous as his Clemency.' An armour-bearer was personal bodyguard to a chief, a man, Martin tells us, 'whose Business' was to attend on 'the Person of his Master night and day to prevent any Surprize.' In the past, every chief had a 'bold Armour-Bearer' – but that world was vanishing.

The basket-hilt – 'a broad Sword which they call a Clymore', writes John Campbell in his *Description of the Highlanders* (1752) – continued to be the main weapon of well-to-do Highlanders. A single 'Stroke' of the claymore, Campbell adds, 'delivered from one of their Hands, would be sufficient to chop off the Head of the strongest Champion that ever lived.' Despite the Victorian stereotype of the Jacobite Highlander being a man armed with a broadsword and targe, it is striking that whereas Cumberland's redcoats collected 2,320 firelocks from the battlefield at Culloden, they found only 190 swords.

Some Highlanders did, however, have both sword and targe, the latter being an item, Campbell avers, 'so strong that no Ball can penetrate it'. In its design the targe had not changed substantially since the days of Montrose, though fewer of them were now used. Lord George Murray, a veteran of the 1715, 1719 and 1745 rebellions, probably owed his life to a targe, which was nicked with two or three bullets during a skirmish in 1745 with dragoons near the village of Clifton, close to Penrith. Murray recalls that the musket balls 'were so thick about me, that I felt them hot about my head, and I thought some of them went through my hair, which was about two inches long, my bonnet having fallen off'. Murray's targe had actually been lent to him by John Gordon of Glenbucket; few men had their own – in a list of eighty men of the Clanranald regiment, only seven men had one.

Dirks, pistols, muskets (the Jacobite Captain James Johnstone mentions using a blunderbuss at Culloden) and the *sgian dhu* ('black knife') were all typical arms of the nobility and their henchmen. This last weapon was probably not worn in the sock before Victorian times – instead it was *sgian achlais*, the 'armpit knife', so-called (the Englishman Edward Burt noted in the 1730s) because it was kept 'concealed in the Sleeve near the Arm-pit.' Powder for firearms was carried in distinctive horns made

SCOTTISH ARMS AND ARMOUR

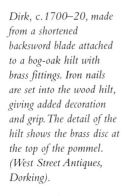

Dirk, c. 1700–20, made from a shortened backsword blade attached to a bog-oak hilt with brass fittings. Iron nails are set into the wood hilt, giving added decoration and grip. The detail of the hilt shows the brass disc at the top of the pommel. (West Street Antiques, Dorking).

from cow horn, flattened by being boiled in water, and sometimes beautifully mounted in silver. Bullets, spare flints and patches for keeping the flint tight in the jaws of the firelock were stored in the *sporan* ('purse').

A LION-HEARTED RABBLE

In battle, the well-armed gentry and their closest retainers formed the front row of the attack. The Hanoverian general Henry 'Hangman' Hawley (d. 1759) calls these men 'True Highlanders', but adds their number was 'always but few'. The main body of fighters behind the 'True Highlanders' was made up of, in Hawley's opinion, 'lowlanders & arrant scum.' Carlyle is more generous, summarising the Jacobite army as 'a Raw Militia, who were not Cowards.' The truth is that in 1689 the men making up the rear of the Jacobite battle-lines were warrior-clansmen liberally armed with spears, Lochaber axes, dirks and bows. In 1745, the rank-and-file were little more than a mob of serving-men, ploughboys, the elderly, even the unemployed and the destitute, with little useful experience and virtually no weapons. At least the Highland gillie had his dirk. Some were lucky enough to be issued with .69-calibre muskets and bayonets from France and Spain; the rest had to plunder, steal or improvise.

The armament of ordinary Jacobites comes across as almost laughably bad in Patrick Crichton of Woodhouselee's account of the occupation of Edinburgh in 1745. To his indignation, Crichton found Edinburgh 'in the keeping of these caterpillars', noticing that the Jacobite army included a 'boy stood with a rusty drawn sword, and two fellows with things licke guns of the 16 centurie', who passed the time by 'catching the vermin from ther lurking places abowt their plaids and throwing them away.' A 'loosie crew' of Jacobites made up of a 'greate many old men and boys' came marching down the street led by their 'mountain officers'. Crichton says this 'rabbell' carried 'guns of different syses, and some of innormowows lengh, some with butts turned up lick a heren [herring] ... some withowt locks and some matchlocks'. Others had 'swords over ther showlder instead of guns, one or two had pitchforks, and some bits of sythes upon poles with a cleek [claw], some old Lochaber axes.' They were so miserably equipped that Crichton wondered if the parade was a 'strategem' to lull the government into thinking the Jacobites were a weak foe, while keeping 'conceiled there best men and arms'. There was no hidden force of elite insurgents: this was the army of the royal house of Stuart.

Knife said to have been used by a Cameron at Culloden, initialled 'D. C.' (West Highland Museum, Fort William)

FAR LEFT
Dirk in leather sheath, dated 1781.
Despite the ban on weapons enacted
after Culloden, dirks continued to be
made in the traditional style.
(The Trustees of the Victoria and
Albert Museum)

CENTRE
Dirk with a blade from an older
broadsword marked with the orb and
cross and running wolf marks for
Solingen, Germany; cut down to size
and set into a high-shouldered hilt of
bog-oak by a Scottish smith,
c.1750–80. (Thomas Del Mar Ltd)

LEFT
Dirk made from a cut-down
backsword blade, with a single fuller
and stamped with maker's mark,
with a plain 'thistle-top' hilt of
turned wood, reinforced with a steel
ring socket, c.1700–70.
(Michael German Antiques)

BELOW
The hilt of the same dirk of 1781,
carved with characteristically
Highland 'basket-weave' interlace.
(The Trustees of the Victoria and
Albert Museum)

Nevertheless, as men the Highlanders were impressive physical specimens. The poet and Hanoverian volunteer John Home (1722–1808) calls those he saw in Edinburgh 'strong, active and hardy men', whose 'stern countenances, and bushy uncombed hair, gave them a fierce, barbarous and imposing aspect'. There was, even in the dying days of clan society, a haughty pride to the Highlander. Campbell says Highlanders were like Venetians: all noble, added to which, all had 'Hearts like Lions.' Charles did have a few well-armed units, notably the regiment of David, Lord Ogilvy (1725–1803), which stood out for its discipline (usually lax in the Jacobite army), as well as for its equipment. Besides, even improvised weapons like scythes were deadly in the hands of lion-hearted Highlanders. MacGregors armed with these makeshift arms wrought havoc among the Hanoverian cavalry at Prestonpans, cleaving and hewing their way through horse and horsemen alike.

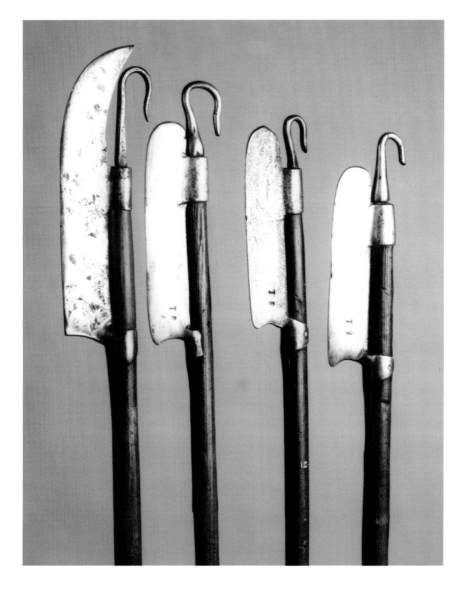

Early eighteenth-century Lochaber axes used by the Edinburgh Town Guard. (The Trustees of the National Museum of Scotland)

Once his blood was up, not even cavalry could stop the Highlander. At Falkirk (1746) Hawley gave an order amounting to a death sentence when he ordered 700 dragoons to charge 4,000 enthusiastic Highlanders. The Chevalier Johnstone, a Jacobite officer, recalls how the Highlanders lay down on the ground as the dragoons approached and 'thrust their dirks into the bellies of the horses.' It was a standard reaction of Highlanders when up against cavalry to go first for the horse, Johnstone saying that the Highlanders at Falkirk 'enjoined to aim at the noses of the horses with their swords, without minding the riders'. Then came the turn of the riders, and as Johnstone recounts, the dragoons were seized by their clothes, dragged from their injured horses, and set upon with dirks, bayonets, axes and guns fired at point-blank range.

'MAKE BUT A BREAKFAST OF OUR MEN'

This terrifying, bloodthirsty fearlessness, this quick-witted recklessness, proved, for a time, a more powerful weapon than the musketry and drill of the Hanoverians. At Prestonpans the Camerons showed great tactical decision-making by making straight for the Hanoverian artillery train, which they overran in seconds. Government soldiers must have died at a rate of something like one a second at Prestonpans, regardless of the shortage of swords and guns. The Jacobites, in contrast, lost about thirty men. At Falkirk, four to five hundred redcoats were slain in half an hour in return for fifty or so Jacobite souls. Hawley complained to Cumberland that his army at Falkirk was guilty of 'scandalous Cowardice', that the 'whole second line of Foot ran away without firing a Shot.' One of those who held his ground was Sir Robert Munro, Colonel of the 37th Regiment. His son describes his last moments:

> My father, after being deserted, was attacked by six of [Cameron of] Locheal's Regt, and for some time he defended himself wt his half Pike. Two of the six, I'm inform'd he kill'd; a seventh, coming up, fired a Pistol into my father's Groin; upon wch falling, the Highlander wh his sword gave him two strokes in the face, over the Eyes & another on the mouth, wch instantly ended a brave Man.

Carlyle conveys the atmosphere of trepidation among the Hanoverian militia as rumours spread like wildfire of 'how numerous and Fierce the Highlanders were, how keen for the Fight, and how they would make but a Breakfast of our Men.' This reputation was entirely justified, and the startling Gaelic bullishness pervaded the laird as much as the common clansmen. Carlyle did not forget his encounter with the young David, Lord Elcho, commander of Prince Charles's Lifeguards, who:

> ... pass'd with his Train, and had an air of Savage Ferocity, that Disgusted and alarm'd – He enquir'd fiercely of me, Where a publick House was to be found; I answer'd him very meekly, not Doubting but that If I had Displeas'd him with my Tone, his Reply would have been with a Pistol Bullet.

UNIFORMS OF THE 'FORTY-FIVE

The symbol of the Jacobite movement was the white cockade, which every rebel wore. Most Jacobites dressed in tartan, usually their own, in line with a decision made by the rebel command to attempt to clothe the entire army in tartan, whatever their cultural origins – a shrewd decision given the terror Highlanders generated. Charles himself was 'clad as an ordinary Captain', writes Andrew Henderson, who saw the Prince at Prestonpans, and states his dress to have been 'a coarse Plaid and blue Bonnet'. Henderson, a Whig sympathiser, cannot resist the mischievous observation: 'his Boots and Knees were much dirtied; he seemed to have fallen into a Ditch, which I was told by one of his Lifeguards he had.'

There were exceptions to the tartan rule. Lord Elcho's 150 Lifeguards, all gentlemen (with an English standard-bearer, Captain John Daniel) and 'all extremely well mounted', wore fine uniforms of 'blew and reed'. Also in standardised uniforms were the Royal Ecossois who came over from France for the 'Forty-Five. They had been raised in 1743 by Lord John Drummond, and their uniform is described by a witness at the trial of one of their officers, a man named Lieutenant

Backsword, hilt of pierced iron, made by a member of the Allan family of Stirling, c. 1730 (The Trustees of the Victoria and Albert Museum).

A highly superior broadsword of c. 1700–20. Its hilt is Scottish, its blade an older German piece from the late seventeenth century, with tooled leather scabbard. The sword formerly belonged to Gina Campbell, who inherited it from her father, the racing driver Donald Campbell. He received it from his father Sir Malcolm Campbell with the tradition that it was used by a Campbell ancestor at Culloden. (West Street Antiques, Dorking)

Charles Oliphant: 'Prisoner wore the uniform of Lord John Drummond's officers, viz; short blue coats, red vests laced with bonnets and white cockades.'

The Irish Brigade was another exception. They too had come over from France for the campaign, 1,100 men of them in redcoats, styled 'piquets', under the talented leadership of Lieutenant Colonel Walter Stapleton. Many other Scots and Irish exiles travelled over from France for the rising: detachments of FitzJames' Horse were landed in Scotland under the command of Robert O'Shea, and were unique among the Jacobites for their cuirasses (which they promptly cast aside). Other cavalry were provided by John Murray of Broughton, who raised a troop of hussars dressed in tartan waistcoats, shoulder plaids, fur-caps and armed with 'Turkish' scimitar-bladed claymores. Lord Kilmarnock from the Lowlands and Lord Pitsligo both commanded contingents of cavalry, though by the time of Culloden most of the horses were dead or starving, and Kilmarnock's squadron was reformed as infantry. These units gave the Jacobites of 1745–6 a semblance of being a conventional eighteenth-century army. All the cavalrymen were well armed with swords and guns, and so too were the uniformed infantry of the Jacobite host, with muskets, swords and bayonets.

The Campbell broadsword in its entirety. (West Street Antiques, Dorking)

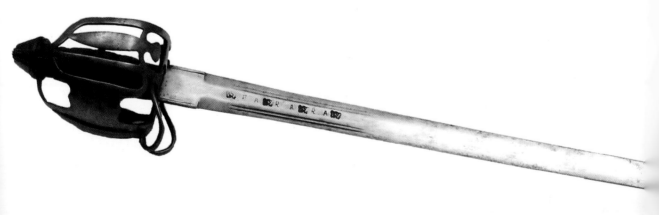

CULLODEN

The Jacobite cause died at a lonely, rain-soaked place called Culloden, near Inverness, on 16 April 1746. Prestonpans, Falkirk and the Jacobite invasion of England had led Charles to believe that his Highlanders were invincible. They were not, of course, and commanding the government forces at Culloden was William Augustus, Duke of Cumberland, a far more skilful (and brutal) general than the Jacobites had ever faced before. Cumberland's troops included large numbers of Scotsmen, indeed large numbers of Highlanders. Some were in the regular army, while the Clan Campbell provided the Hanoverians with the same kind of wild muscle that had served Charles so well.

Culloden was also the first occasion that a Jacobite army had been exposed to well-deployed artillery. Cannon heralded the opening of the battle. The Jacobite artillerymen, spirited but amateurish, were no match for Cumberland's professional gunners. The government artillery tore holes in the Jacobite lines, causing the rebels to surge forwards in a flustered, chaotic attack. Cumberland's dispatch says the Jacobites 'came running on in their wild manner … firing their pistols and

Blade of the Campbell claymore, signed on one side 'Andrea', the other 'Farara'. Scottish swords are often signed with the name of Andrea Ferrara, a sixteenth-century Italian swordsmith, but later Germans made blades bearing his name. This was taken by Scots as a sign of quality rather than an attempt to deceive, though some Highlanders may have thought Ferrara was a Spaniard, for Gaelic poetry and song often mentions 'Spanish' blades. (West Street Antiques, Dorking)

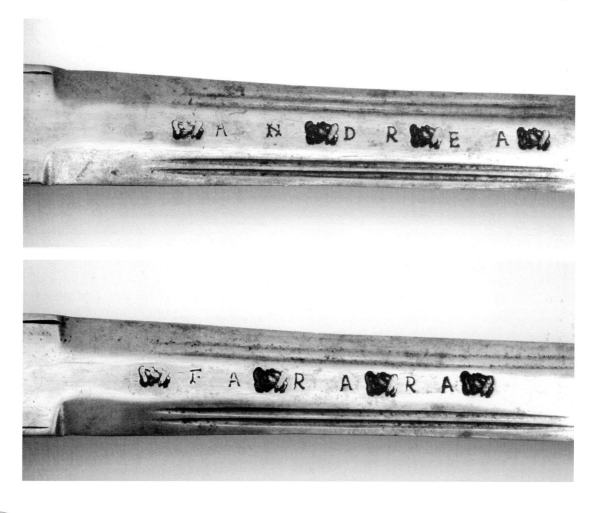

The Campbell broadsword has fish-skin grips bound with wire. (West Street Antiques, Dorking)

brandishing their Swords' – but the redcoats, with true Scottish and English grit, held firm and fired one steady volley after another. The Jacobite attack stalled and Charles' staff panicked, imploring their prince to retreat. The Marquis d'Eguilles, French ambassador to Charles's 'court', remembers the prince's sudden transformation from 'Bonnie Prince Charlie' into 'the most striking spectacle of human weakness' he had ever seen. The prince, D'Eguilles writes, 'was vanquished in an instant, never was a defeat more complete than his.' As his men made desperate attempts to hold back Cumberland's advance, Charles and his entourage withdrew from the battlefield. The fate of the Jacobite army was sealed.

Later in life, Charles would wish he had died with his Highlanders at Culloden. It was not only many of his Jacobites that had perished, but a whole way of life. After Culloden, Cumberland's men ruthlessly harried the Highlands. Later in 1746 a Disclothing Act was passed by Westminster decreeing that, on pain of seven years' transportation, 'no man or boy within that part of Britain called Scotland ... shall, on any pretext whatever, wear or put on the clothes commonly called Highland clothes (that is to say) the Plaid, Philabeg, or little Kilt, Trowse, Shoulder-belts ... that no tartan or party coloured plaid of stuff shall be used for Great Coats or upper coats.' In 1747 a new, harsher disarming law known as the Act of Proscription came into force. Highland dress and weaponry were outlawed by the government precisely because they knew them to be the sacred bedrock of clanship. It now seemed impossible that Scottish arms and armour would survive.

Chapter Seven

A NEW SCOTLAND

THE PROSCRIPTION ACT almost succeeded in killing Scottish arms, armour and costume. Only in the army did they survive. But in the army claymores, dirks and kilts were produced to regulated patterns, so that when the acts against wearing Highland dress were repealed in 1782 the resurrected, reconstituted style of arms and armour had a military, 'standard issue' look about it. Even so, while salaried colonels took the place of chiefs, a sense of clanship was successfully fostered and preserved among the Highland regiments. Bagpipes were still – and remain – the heart and soul of a Scottish unit.

THE RAISING OF THE HIGHLAND REGIMENTS

The first regiment of the British Army to wear tartan (a dark sett named 'Government' or 'Universal,' with pipers later wearing Royal Stewart) was the 'Black Watch,' raised in 1739. At that time Lowland units wore uniforms like any other line regiment of the British Army. By the time the Cameron Highlanders were established in 1793, a sentimental, escapist craze for 'Celtic' culture was sweeping the British Isles. Jacobite insurgency was safely in the past and Bonnie Prince Charlie, who died a broken drunk at Rome in 1788, could be celebrated fondly – even by Hanoverians – as a wonderfully doomed hero of another age. A catalyst for the revival

Claymore, c.1780–1800.(By kind permission of the Masters of the Bench of the Honourable Society of the Middle Temple).

Major-General Sir Evan
MacGregor, Chief of the
MacGregors, on the
occasion of George IV's
visit to Edinburgh in
1822. (Private collection)

of earlier, native forms of Scottish arms, albeit in heavily sanitised form, was the royal visit to Edinburgh in 1822 by a tartan-clad George IV. Scotland received George – the first British monarch to set foot on Scottish soil since Charles II – with much gaudy pomp and parades of clan 'armies' led by their chiefs, all carefully stage-managed by Sir Walter Scott. Not having enough weapons to arm their clansmen, the Board of Ordnance had to lend swords for the occasion, as they did again in 1842 for Victoria and Albert's first visit to Scotland.

Proud of her Stuart ancestry, Queen Victoria (reigned 1837–1901) fell in love with the Highlands, for though its clan system and age-old way of life were gone, the region still retained, for outsiders at least, an aura of masculine legend and mystery. The achievement of the Victorians was their transformation of what was once specifically Highland dress into a national costume for all Scots, realigning the kilt (lengthened to reach the knee to preserve Victorian modesty) and its attendant articles as emblems of patriotic British Unionism. The reality was that many of the necessary items were being produced in English cities. Wilkinson of London and cutlers in Sheffield saw their chance and made blades for claymores and dirks. Isaac Bissell and John Waters of Birmingham churned out rather bad but very cheap pistols for the army and private market.

Dirks were made in Birmingham too, and cutlers and jewellers in London made and sold a wide range of Highland costume accessories. But craftsmen in Scotland also began making dirks, claymores, *sgian dhus*, pistols, kilts, targes, brooches, kilt-pins, bonnets and powder horns again. While many beautiful pieces were made

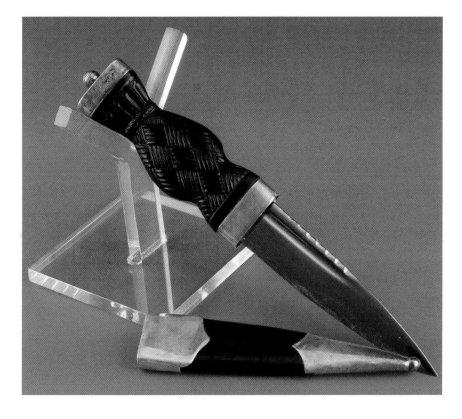

Sgian dhu *with silver mounts*, c. 1890. *(Michael German Antiques)*

during the nineteenth and twentieth centuries, Scottish arms and armour had generally lost its earthy ruggedness. The Victorians managed to bring back wappinschaws in the 1850s, but Scottish arms and dress had become, by and large, the contrived stuff of social functions, parades and balls, rather than battles.

THE SPREAD OF HIGHLAND ARMS AND ARMOUR

On the battlefield, however, the sight of massed Highlanders in kilts still inspired an awe and respect that other uniforms could not. Valiant and loyal service in the Seven Years' War, Napoleonic Wars, the Crimea, the Boer Wars and many other conflicts across the British Empire brought Highlanders enormous fame and prestige. Lowland regiments were soon enthusiastically adopting tartan, the Army Reforms of 1881 putting Lowland regiments into semi-Highland dress of trews. The power

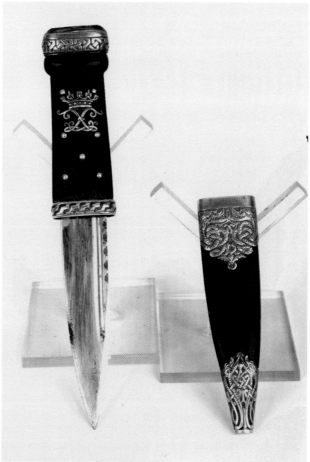

ABOVE LEFT AND LEFT
*Dirk, with silver mounts set
with cairngorms, c. 1900.
(Michael German Antiques)*

ABOVE
Sgian dhu *with silver mounts,
c. 1900. (Michael German
Antiques)*

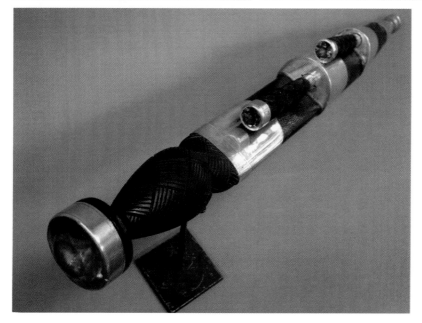

Sgian dhu *with silver mounts set with a cairngorm, c. 1895. (Michael German Antiques)*

Queen Victoria was profoundly fond of the Highlands and its people. Here, towards the end of her reign, she is attended by two Highlanders as she processes through London. The future Edward VII rides along behind. (John Wesley's House and the Museum of Methodism)

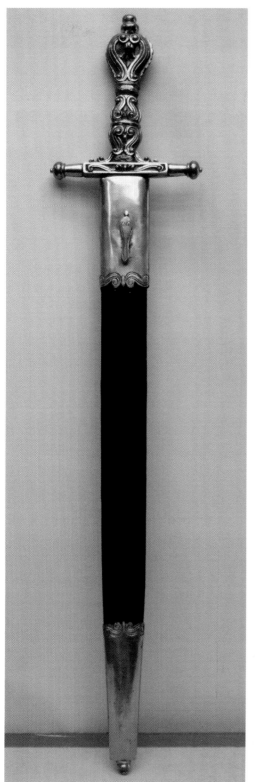

FAR LEFT
Field dress sword for a Gentleman of the Royal Company of Archers, c. 1860. Blade marked 'Holbeck & Sons 4 New Bond Street London.' Founded in 1676, the Company of Archers are the Queen's bodyguard in Scotland. (Michael German Antiques)

ABOVE
Boy's sgian dhu, *mounted with silver, c. 1900. (Michael German Antiques)*

LEFT
Sgian dhu *with silver mounts, c. 1890. (Michael German Antiques)*

ABOVE
Alexander Calder joined the
London Scottish in 1910 and
took part in the unit's bayonet
charge at Messines.
Commissioned into the Argyll
and Sutherland Highlanders,
Calder won the Military
Cross. He was killed at the
Somme in 1916. (All three
pictures London Scottish
Regimental Trust)

ABOVE RIGHT
Three privates of the London
Scottish in France, 1917.

RIGHT
Survivors of the 1st Battalion
London Scottish the day after
the battle of Messines, fought
on Halloween, 1914.

of Highland dress was so great that men of Scots origin around the world, driven from their homeland by war, clearances and the chance of a more prosperous future, sought to recreate a little piece of Caledonia in their own armies, establishing such units as the Cape Town Highlanders (1885) and the Toronto Scottish (1920). The same was true in England. The London Scottish, dressed in hodden grey, was formed in 1859, followed by the Liverpool Scottish (1900), Manchester Scottish (1914) and Tyneside Scottish (1914).

These units of Scottish 'exiles' served in the First World War. Anyone drunk on the romance of Scottish arms and armour will be sobered up by the reality of the 1914–18 war. While an accurate tally of Scottish dead does not exist, of 690,235 Scots mobilised for the war perhaps 20 per cent were killed. At least as many again were wounded, many so severely that they were permanently disabled. Just about every community in Scotland, however small, has its memorial to local dead. The Royal Scots alone suffered 11,213 casualties; the Black Watch and Highland Light Infantry lost 10,000 men each; the Gordons lost 9,000; 30 Scottish international rugby players were among the war dead. We must never forget that the express purpose of nearly every object in this book was to kill and destroy. Even those made for ceremonial use are still based on tools designed to inflict harm. We may appreciate their design and decoration, but – put simply – there is no craftsmanship to the visceral misery of war, whether at the Somme, Culloden, Flodden or Mons Graupius.

Sgian dhu, *mounted with silver and a cairngorm, c. 1900. (Michael German Antiques)*

SCOTTISH ARMS AND ARMOUR TODAY

Scottish military dress, of all periods, activates and excites something primitive and animalistic in our psyche, and there is no more magnificent spectacle than Scottish soldiers on parade. In the present age the Scottish martial tradition burns bright but faces new challenges. In 2006, following a controversial amalgamation of units, the title 'Highlanders' disappeared from the British Army's list of infantry regiments after 266 years. The following year it was reported that the Royal Regiment of Scotland have been short of kilts. Yet even these changes cannot prevent the continued life of arms and armour in Scotland. Dirks, *sgian dhus* and claymores are still made and still worn at formal occasions by soldiers and civilians alike, ensuring that, even after the 10,000 years of human history we have travelled through in this book, arms and armour remain living elements of Scottish nationhood.

FURTHER READING

GENERAL

Bezdek, R. H. *Swords and Sword Makers of England and Scotland.* Paladin, 2003.

Caldwell, D. H. (editor) *Scottish Weapons and Fortifications, 1100–1800.* John Donald, 1981.

Drummond, J. and Anderson, J. *Ancient Scottish Weapons.* Waterson and Sons, 1881.

Dunbar, J. T. *History of Highland Dress: A Definitive Study of the History of Scottish Costume and Tartan, Both Civil and Military, Including Weapons.* Oliver and Boyd, 1979.

Hume Brown, P. (editor) *Early Travellers in Scotland.* Burt Franklin, 1970.

McClintock, H. F. *Old Irish and Highland Dress*, 2nd edn. W. Tempest, 1949.

McIan, R. R. and Logan, J. *The Clans of the Scottish Highlands: The Costumes of the Clans.* Chancellor Press, 1983.

Newark, T. *Celtic Warriors 400 BC–AD 1600.* Blandford, 1986.

THE ANCIENT PERIOD

Alcock, L. *The Neighbours of the Picts: Angles, Britons and Scots at War and at Home.* Dornoch, 1993.

Allen, S. *Celtic Warrior.* Osprey, 2001.

Allen, S. *Lords of Battle: The World of the Celtic Warrior.* Osprey, 2007.

Armit, I. *Celtic Scotland.* RCAHMS and Batsford, 1997.

Connolly, P. *Greece and Rome at War.* Macdonald, 1981.

Cunliffe, B. *Iron Age Britain.* English Heritage, 1995.

Foster, S. M. *Picts, Gaels and Scots: Early Historic Scotland.* RCAHMS and Batsford, 1996.

James, S. *Exploring the World of the Celts*, 2nd edn. Thames and Hudson, 2005.

James, S. and Rigby, V. *Britain and the Celtic Iron Age.* British Museum, 1997.

Laing, L. *Later Celtic Art in Britain and Ireland*, 2nd edn. Shire, 1997.

Megaw, R. and V. *Early Celtic Art in Britain and Ireland.* Shire, 1986.

Pleiner, R. *The Celtic Sword.* Clarendon, 1993.

Pryor, F. *Britain BC: Life in Britain and Ireland Before the Romans.* Harper Collins, 2003.

Ritchie, W. and J. *Celtic Warriors.* Shire, 1985.

Smyth, A. P. *Warlords and Holymen: Scotland AD 80–1000.* Edward Arnold, 1984.

Wilcox, P. *Rome's Enemies (2): Gallic and British Celts.* Osprey, 1985.

THE MIDDLE AGES

Anderson, A. O. (editor) *Scottish Annals from English Chroniclers AD 500–1286.* D. N. Nutt, 1908.

Armstrong, P. *Stirling Bridge and Falkirk 1297–98: William Wallace's Rebellion.* Osprey, 2003.

Armstrong, P. *Otterburn 1388: Bloody Border Conflict.* Osprey, 2006.

Barbour, John (translated and edited by A. A. M. Duncan). *The Bruce.* Canongate, 1997.

Barr, N. *Flodden*, 2nd edn. Tempus, 2003.

Barrow, G. W. S. *Robert Bruce and the Community of the Realm of Scotland.* Edinburgh University Press, 1965.

Barrow, G. W. S. *Kingship and Unity: Scotland 1000–1306*. Edward Arnold, 1981.

Boece, Hector (edited by G. Watson). *The Mar Lodge Translation of the History of Scotland*. Scottish Text Society, 1946.

Bourke, C. 'Antiquities from the River Blackwater III, Iron Axe-Heads', in *Ulster Journal of Archaeology*, 3rd series, 60. 2001.

Bower, Walter (translated and edited by D. E. R. Watt). *Scotichronicon*. Aberdeen University Press, 1987–98 (9 vols).

Buchannan, George (translated and edited by J. Aitken). *The History of Scotland*. Blackie, Fullarton and Co., 1827–9 (6 vols).

Caldwell, D. 'Claymores – The Two-Handed Swords of the Scottish Highlanders', in *Park Lane Arms Fair*. 2005.

Campbell Patterson, R. *My Wound is Deep: A History of the Later Anglo-Scots Wars 1380–1560*. John Donald, 1997.

Cannan, F. *Galloglass 1250–1600*. Osprey, 2009.

Denholm-Young, N. (translator and editor) *Vita Edwardi Secundi*. Thomas Nelson and Sons, 1957.

Duffy, S. (editor) *Robert the Bruce's Irish Wars: The Invasions of Ireland 1306–1329*. Tempus, 2002.

Duffy, S. (editor) *The World of the Galloglass: Kings, Warlords and Warriors in Ireland and Scotland, 1200–1600*. Four Courts, 2007.

Durham, K. *The Border Reivers*. Osprey, 1995.

Fisher, A. *William Wallace*. John Donald, 1986.

John of Fordun (translated and edited by W. F. and F. J. H. Skene). 'Chronicle of the Scottish Nation', in *Historians of Scotland*, vol. 4, 1872 (2 vols).

Froissart, Jean (translated and edited by G. Brereton). *Chronicles*, 2nd edn. Penguin Classics, 1978.

Hannay, R. K. (editor) *Acts of the Lords of Council in Public Affairs, 1501–1554*. Register House, 1932.

Harbison, P. 'Native Irish Arms and Armour in Medieval Gaelic Literature, 1170–1600', in *The Irish Sword*, part 1: 12. 1975; part 2: 13. 1976.

Hayes-McCoy, G. A. *Scots Mercenary Forces in Ireland 1565–1603*. Burns, Oates and Co., 1937.

Hayes-McCoy, G. A. 'The Gallóglach Axe', in *Journal of the Galway Archaeological and Historical Society*, 17, 1937.

Lesley, John (translated and edited by T. Thompson). *The History of Scotland from the Death of King James I in the Year 1436 to the Year 1561*. Bannatyne Club, 1830.

Lindsay of Pitscottie, Robert (edited by Æ. J. E. MacKay). *The Historie and Cronicles of Scotland*. Scottish Texts Society, 1899–1911 (3 vols).

Major, John (translated and edited by Æ. J. H. Mackay). *A History of Greater Britain*. Scottish History Society, 1892.

Maxwell, H. (translator and editor) *The Chronicle of Lanercost, 1272–1346*. Maclehose and Sons, 1913.

McKerral, A. 'West Highland Mercenaries in Ireland', in *Scottish Historical Review*, 30, 1951.

McNamee, C. *The Wars of the Bruces: Scotland, England and Ireland, 1306–1328*. Tuckwell, 1997.

Skene, F. J. H. (editor) 'The Book of Pluscarden' in *The Historians of Scotland*, vol. 10, 1880 (2 vols).

Steer, K. A. and Bannerman, J. W. M. *Late Medieval Monumental Sculpture in the West Highlands*.

RCAHMS, 1977.

Thomson, T. and Innes, C. (editors) *The Acts of the Parliament of Scotland*. HM Stationery Office, 1814–75, 12 vols.

Willis, T. 'Scottish "Twa Handit Swerdis"', in *Park Lane Arms Fair*. 1996.

Andrew of Wyntoun (edited by F. J. Amours). *The Original Chronicle*. Scottish Text Society, 1908 (6 vols).

GAELIC BLACKSMITHS AND 'MEN OF ART'

Campbell, A. *A History of Clan Campbell, vol. 1: From Origins to Flodden*. Polygon, 2000.

Campbell, J. F. *Popular Tales of the West Highlands Orally Collected*. Edmonston and Douglas, 1860 (4 vols).

Cheape, H. 'Clanranald's Blacksmith', in *Clan Donald Magazine*, 12. 1991.

Grant, K. W. *Myth, Tradition and Story from Western Argyll*. Oban Times Press, 1925.

King, R. 'The Clanranald Anvil: Where Did All the Wood Come From?', in *The Urcheon*, 3. Winter edition 2008.

Martin, Martin. *A Description of the Western Isles of Scotland circa 1695 and a Late Voyage to St Kilda; Description of the Occidental i.e. Western Isles of Scotland by Donald Munro*. Birlinn, 1999.

McOwan, R. 'Dirks from Dalmally', in *The Scots Magazine*. August 1991.

Nicolson, A. (edited by A. Maclean) *History of Skye: A Record of the Families, The Social Conditions and The Literature of the Island*, 2nd edn. Maclean Press, 1994.

Scott, B. G. *Early Irish Ironworking*. Ulster Museum Publications, 1990.

Steer, K. A. and Bannerman, J. W. M. *Late Medieval Monumental Sculpture in the West Highlands*. RCAHMS, 1977.

Thomson, D. S. 'Gaelic Learned Orders and Literati in Medieval Scotland', in *Scottish Studies*, 12, part 1. 1968.

FIREARMS AND THE LOWLAND AND BURGH ARMAMENTS INDUSTRY

Blair, C., and Woosnam-Savage, R. *Scottish Firearms*. Museum Restoration Service, 1995.

Caldwell, D. H. 'Royal Patronage of Arms and Armour Making in Fifteenth and Sixteenth Century Scotland', in Caldwell, D. H. (editor) *Scottish Weapons and Fortifications, 1100–1800*. John Donald, 1981.

Caldwell, D. H. 'Scottish Pistols: A Celtic Style?', in *Dispatch*, 103. 1983.

Caldwell, D. H. 'The Art of Scottish Firearms', in *Man at Arms*. January–February 1985.

Caldwell, D. H. 'The Lutiger Gun Barrel and the Manufacture of Long Guns in 16th-Century Scotland', in *Park Lane Arms Fair*. 1987.

Caldwell, D. H. 'Scottish Powder-Horns', in *Park Lane Arms Fair*. 1989.

Caldwell, D. H. 'Scottish Traditional Gunmaking', in *The Journal of the Antique Metalware Society*. 13 June 2005.

Gaier, C. 'The Origin of Mons Meg', in *Journal of the Arms and Armour Society*, 5. 1967.

MacDougall, N. *James IV*. Tuckwell, 1989.

MacDougall, N. '"The Greatest Scheip That Ewer Saillit in England or France": James IV's "Great Michael"', in *Scotland and War AD 79–1918*. John Donald, 1991.

Kelvin, M. *The Scottish Pistol, its History, Design and Manufacture*. Cygnus Arts, 1996.

Norman, A. V. B. 'The John Simpsons of Glasgow', in *Dispatch: The Journal of the Scottish Military*

History Society, 131. Spring 1993.

Oliver, D. 'John Allan of Stirling', in *Park Lane Arms Fair*. 2000.

Paul, J. B. et al. (editors) *Accounts of the Lord High Treasurer of Scotland*. HM Stationery Office, 1877–1978 (12 vols).

Stevenson, D. and Caldwell, D. H. 'Leather Guns and Other Light Artillery in Mid-17th-Century Scotland', in *Proceedings of the Society of Antiquaries of Scotland*, vol. 108. 1976–7.

Whitelaw, C. 'A Treatise on Scottish Hand Firearms', in H. J. Jackson, *European Hand Firearms of the Sixteenth, Seventeenth and Eighteenth Centuries*. P. L. Warner, 1923.

Whitelaw, C. (edited by S. Barter) *Scottish Arms Makers: A Biographical Dictionary of Makers of Firearms, Edged Weapons and Armour, Working in Scotland from the 15th Century to 1870*. Arms and Armour Press, 1977.

FROM THE UNION OF 1603 TO CULLODEN

Mackenzie, R., Cheape, H., Norman, A. V. B., Batty, J., Moran, J., Foster, G., and Holloway, J. *Culloden – The Swords and the Sorrows: An Exhibition to Commemorate the Jacobite Rising of 1745 and the Battle of Culloden in 1746*. National Trust for Scotland, 1996.

Blair, C., and Wallace, J. 'Scots or English?', in *Scottish Arts Review*, Special Number, 9. 1963.

Blair, C. 'The Word Claymore and Other Gaelic Sword Terms', in *The Journal of the Arms and Armour Society*, 16, no. 1. September 1998.

Boswell, James. *The Journal of a Tour to the Hebrides with Samuel Johnson*. Everyman, 1931.

Brown, I. A. and Cheape, H. *Witness to Rebellion: John Maclean's Journal of the Forty-Five and the Penicuik Drawings*. Tuckwell and National Library of Scotland, 1996.

Carlyle, Alexander. *Anecdotes and Characters of the Times*, ed. J. Kinsley. Oxford English Memoirs and Travels, 1973.

Chambers, R. *Jacobite Memoirs of the Rebellion of 1745*. Chambers, 1834 (includes Lord George Murray's 'Marches of the Highland Army').

Dalgleish, G. and Mechan, D. *I Am Come Home*. National Museums of Scotland, 1985.

Dalton, C. *The Scots Army 1661–1688*. Greenhill and Presidio, 1989.

Drummond, John (edited by J. MacKnight). *Memoirs of Sir Ewen Cameron of Locheill: Chief of the Clan Cameron*. Maitland Club, 1842.

Drummond, J. *Highland Targets and Other Shields*. Neill and Company, 1873.

Elcho, David (edited by E. Charteris). *A Short Account of the Affairs of Scotland in the Years 1744, 1745, 1746*. David Douglas, 1907.

Elder, J. R. *The Highland Host of 1678*. James Maclehose and Sons, 1914.

Forbes, Robert (edited by H. Paton). *The Lyon in Mourning*. Scottish History Society, 1895–6 (3 vols).

Furgol, E. M. *A Regimental History of the Covenanting Armies, 1639–1651*. John Donald, 1990.

Jenner, H. and Robinson, F. E. (editors) *Memoirs of the Lord Viscount Dundee, The Highland Clans and the Massacre at Glencoe*. 1908.

Johnstone, Chevalier de (translated by C. Winchester). *Memoirs*. D. Wyllie, 1870.

Kenyon, J. and Ohlmeyer J. (editors) *The Civil Wars: A Military History of England, Scotland and Ireland 1638–1660*. Oxford University Press, 1998.

Kelvin, M. *Jacobite Legacy: A Catalogue of Memorabilia of the Jacobite Era*. G. C. Books, 2003.

Mackay, Hugh (edited by J. M. Hog, P. F. Tytler and A. Urquhart). *Memoirs of the War Carried On in Scotland and Ireland 1689–91*. Bannatyne Club, 1833.

McLynn, F. *Bonnie Prince Charlie: Charles Edward Stuart*, 3rd edn. Pimlico, 2003.

Norman, A. V. B. 'Prince Charles Edward's Silver-Hilted Sword', in *The Proceedings of the Society of Antiquaries of Scotland*, 108. 1976–7.

Reid, S. *Like Hungry Wolves: Culloden Moor 16 April 1746*. Windrow and Greene, 1994.

Reid, S. *Highland Clansman 1689–1746*. Osprey, 1997.

Reid, S. *Auldearn 1645: The Marquis of Montrose's Scottish Campaign*. Osprey, 2003.

Reid, S. *Dunbar 1650: Cromwell's Most Famous Victory*. Osprey, 2004.

Scott, A. M. *Bonnie Dundee*. John Donald, 1989.

Sinclair, John (edited by J. MacKnight and D. Laing). *Memoirs of the Insurrection in Scotland in 1715*. Abbotsford Club, 1858.

Tomasson, K. and Buist, F. *Battles of the '45*. Batsford, 1967.

Wishart, George (translated and edited by A. D. Murdoch and H. F. M. Simpson). *The Memoirs of James, Marquis of Montrose, 1639–1650*. Longmans, Green, 1893.

AFTER CULLODEN TO THE PRESENT AGE

Anderson, D. N. *Scots in Uniform: The Military Costume of Scotland's Horse and Foot*. Holmes McDougall, 1972.

Barnes, R. M. *The Uniforms and History of the Scottish Regiments: Britain, Canada, Australia, New Zealand, South Africa 1625 to the Present Day*. Imperial Services Library, vol. 2, 1960.

Caldwell, D. H. 'Highland Armies of the 19th Century', in *The Highlander*, 26, 1. January–February 1988.

Caldwell, D. H. 'Traditional Scottish Weapons – The Last Phases', in *Park Lane Arms Fair*. 1998.

Chappell, M. *Scottish Units in the World Wars*. Osprey, 1994.

Cochrane, P. *Scottish Military Dress*. Blandford, 1987.

Reid, S. *Queen Victoria's Highlanders*. Osprey, 2007.

Royle, T. *The Flowers of the Forest: Scotland and the First World War*. Birlinn, 2006.

Wilkinson-Latham, R. *Scottish Military Uniforms*. David and Charles, 1975.

PLACES TO VISIT

Anyone interested in Scottish arms and armour should visit the National Museum of Scotland in Edinburgh and Glasgow Art Gallery and Museum. For a real treat go to the West Highland Museum in Fort William, where a wonderful miscellany of objects gives the visitor a real feel for the world of the Highland warrior. The world of the galloglass and 'redshank' fighter in Ireland can be grasped by going to the Ulster Museum, Belfast, and Collins Barracks branch of the National Museum of Ireland, Dublin. For the period post-Culloden, the Scottish War Museum in Edinburgh is well worth visiting. Many castles, stately homes and local museums in Scotland, such as Dean Castle, Kilmarnock and Dumfries Museum, contain exciting material. Those wanting to see portraiture featuring arms and armour should make for the Scottish National Portrait Gallery in Edinburgh. In London, the British Museum has strong collections relating to the ancient Celts, and the Victoria and Albert Museum has some good Scottish weapons (in store at the time of writing), as does the Royal Armouries in Leeds.

INDEX

Page numbers in italic refer to illustrations

INDEX

Page numbers in italic refer to illustrations